SCOTLAND'S FAR WEST

Philip Hinchliffe   *Denis Brook*

About the Authors

Denis Brook and Phil Hinchliffe, now retired, were born and educated in Huddersfield. They became electrical engineers, Denis (after a period in R&D) lecturing at the then Huddersfield Polytechnic and Phil working for the BBC. They have walked extensively in the north of England and the Highlands of Scotland. They have trekked in Nepal, Peru and India and made ascents of Mts Kenya, Kilimanjaro and Stok Kangri, a 6153m (20,181ft) peak in Ladakh.

Other Cicerone guidebooks by the authors
North to the Cape

SCOTLAND'S FAR WEST

Walks on the Isle of Mull and Ardnamurchan

by

Denis Brook and Phil Hinchliffe

CICERONE

2 POLICE SQUARE, MILNTHORPE, CUMBRIA LA7 7PY
www.cicerone.co.uk

First edition 2005, reprinted 2010
ISBN-10: 1 85284 407 8
ISBN-13: 978 1 85284 407 3

Printed by KHL Printing, Singapore
A catalogue record for this book is available from the British Library.

OS Ordnance Survey® This project includes mapping data licensed from Ordnance Survey® with the permission of the Controller of Her Majesty's Stationery Office. © Crown copyright 2010. All rights reserved. Licence number PU100012932

Acknowledgements

Grateful thanks are offered to all those who, in one way or another, have helped with the compilation of this book.

Very special appreciation goes to Sheila Banks, a close friend of both the authors, who read the manuscripts (sometimes several times) and offered valuable advice on syntax and grammar. Her advice and encouragement were invaluable. She was also our chauffeur on some of the research trips – a noteworthy act that helped us a lot. Our thanks go to the Tourist Information Offices who provided information and help with reference sources and accommodation.

Finally, our grateful thanks go to the innumerable hoteliers, restaurateurs, shopkeepers, innkeepers and members of the public who assisted us with advice, directions and encouragement.

Front cover: Looking up Glen Gour (Walk 5: Glen Gour)

CONTENTS

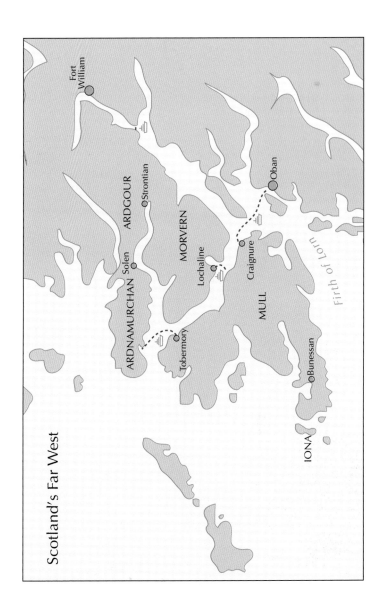

Scotland's Far West

Fort William

Strontian

ARDGOUR

Oban

MORVERN

Solen

Lochaline

Craignure

ARDNAMURCHAN

MULL

Firth of Lorn

Tobermory

Bunessan

IONA

Tree in Glen Clachaig
(Walk 11: Loch Ba to Glen More)

PREFACE

When researching our last guidebook, *North to the Cape*, we spent many happy days in the West Highlands of Scotland, often passing through Fort William on the way to our research destinations.

On one of our trips it occurred to us that, despite our many kilometres afoot, there were two corners of Scotland within reach of Fort William that we had never fully investigated. These were the Isle of Mull and that most westerly part of the British mainland, Ardnamurchan.

So we went on an exploratory visit with no book in mind. We were so enchanted with these places, however, that we soon realised the potential for one. This guide (in which Morvern, Ardgour, Sunart and Ardnamurchan have been grouped, for convenience, under the heading 'Ardnamurchan') is the result of three pleasant years' work and we hope that you will get much pleasure from reading it. We hope too that you will enjoy the walks.

On Mull and on the mainland, we discovered that there are many routes shown on OS maps and published in guides and leaflets. In this guidebook we have chosen the ones we enjoyed the most, and make no excuse for including several walks which might be considered classics, simply because they are too good to miss.

We cover three kinds of walk: circular walks, walks which go out and return at the halfway mark, and those which travel from A to B (linear walks). At the risk of stating the obvious, the linear walks will require pick-up arrangements or a two-car preparation session.

We have described a good mix ranging from easy strolls, which may take half a day or so, to fairly long day walks, including one or two which will stretch your abilities. Fit and experienced walkers should be able to complete all the routes, and we have indicated in the text those areas requiring extra care.

On some walks we have mentioned 'other paths'. Where sensible, destinations of some connecting paths are pointed out, especially at important intersections. We do not expect walkers to slavishly follow our routes step by step. We do expect walkers – as we do – to explore, making full use of maps and navigational skills.

Much has been written elsewhere about the history, natural history and geology of these areas, so we chose not to repeat most of this: after all, this is a guidebook, not a travel book. We have, however, included some information in the introductions to walks where we think it will be of particular interest.

Loch Sunart from Bealach Sloc an Eich (Walk 4: Loch Teacuis to Laudale)

We enjoy walking *in* the countryside, rather than *through* it, tramping around happily rather than trying to break records. We've lost count of the number of days spent in exploring the British Isles, especially the north of England and Scotland. It's not only the walking we enjoy, but also the navigation, mapwork, sorting out a good route, staying in both smart hotels with gourmet food and in more humble establishments. We enjoy the downing of a good pint, perhaps with a dram, in a friendly inn; a wayside chat with a passer-by.

During our walking career, we have visited and been impressed by many magnificent mountain areas around the world. But each time we visit the West Highlands of Scotland and, in particular, Scotland's Far West, we are reminded that this area cannot be surpassed for its hills and glens, its lakes, rivers and lochs, its remoteness and its beauty. For us it remains the best.

Denis Brook and Phil Hinchliffe

GENERAL INFORMATION

GETTING ABOUT

There are bus services available in Scotland's Far West, but they are rural in scope rather than urban, so we recommend the use of private transport to access the walks. Indeed, this is the only way to get to some of them.

In order to utilise your time fully the use of a motor vehicle or motor cycle is essential. Ways of accessing Mull and the mainland are described in the introductions to each area.

Petrol stations are few and far between, so note their location and keep your fuel tank topped up. Remember that some garages may not accept credit cards, and some may not be open on Sundays and/or may have restricted hours in general.

ACCOMMODATION

By their very nature, the walks in this book start and finish in areas where accommodation may be limited or non-existent, hence the need not only for transport but also for carefully planning your overnight stays. You may decide to stay in one centre and do several walks from there, or you may wish to travel around to be as near as possible to a group of walks. We have based the walks in this guidebook on Tobermory, Craignure and Bunessan (near Fionnphort) on Mull, and Lochaline, Strontian and Salen on the mainland, but you can always work out your own itinerary.

On Mull, there is accommodation to suit all tastes in Tobermory and on Iona. There is limited accommodation in Craignure, including a hotel, an inn and the Pennygate Lodge guest house, originally a manse, tucked away behind a garage-cum-shop near the old pier. There is also limited accommodation at Bunessan, as well as in many of the hamlets and villages. On the mainland, Strontian has good accommodation, including the Ben View Hotel, about 1.5km west of the village. There is limited accommodation at Salen and Lochaline and elsewhere. We advise you to make full use of publications listing such facilities and also to use the Tourist Information Centres (TICs – see Appendix II Useful Addresses). Not all accommodation is listed in the publications or registered with the TICs, as evidenced by many roadside notices offering this service.

EQUIPMENT

We would not presume to dictate what to wear and what to put into your rucksack. However, a few comments may be helpful. We recommend that you wear strong, but not heavy, waterproof boots. Unless the weather (see below) is

In Ardnamurchan we came across a very apt sign that sums up our attitude to walking in the hills. It read thus: 'TAKE CARE. You are entering remote, sparsely populated, potentially dangerous mountain country. Please ensure that you are adequately experienced and equipped to complete your journey without assistance.'

exceptionally favourable, you are likely to get wet. We have always been of the opinion that boots are the most important part of any walker's kit; get them wrong and your walk and possibly your physical safety could be in jeopardy.

Bivouac gear (at the least a bivibag) should always be carried in case of an emergency overnight stop. Warm inner clothing and waterproof outer clothing should always be with you; the weather can, and does, change (and worsen) dramatically.

As none of our walks involve (intended) overnight camps, you may neglect to carry emergency rations. This could prove to be a problem if, for whatever reason, any member of your party gets stranded or injured; emergency rations are essential.

Clearly, all mountain walkers should carry a compass and appropriate maps (see 'Maps and navigation' below) and know how to use them. First aid kits should be carried at all times.

MAPS AND NAVIGATION

In this guide, the maps are reproductions from the OS 1:50,000 series with

WALKING POLES

In our early walking careers, the use of poles (or sticks) as walking aids in this country was unknown, except for the elderly or disabled. Now their use is common, even within the younger walking fraternity. They are indispensable for many reasons: providing a third point of support to increase stability; testing boggy or snow-covered ground for softness/hardness and depth; fending off uncooperative dogs and inquisitive cattle or horses; taking the stress off knees, especially when descending; for steadiness when wading across rivers, particularly those with rocky beds, fast-flowing water, or both.

The cost of these advantages is the encumbrance factor. Poles can be a nuisance when scrambling up or down, when both hands are needed, and when operating a camera, especially when taking that quick 'snap'. Despite these restrictions, the use of at least one pole is beneficial. We remain to be convinced of the value of two poles though, as evident out in the hills, some would disagree.

north at the top and, together with the map notes, should be adequate for you to complete any of the walks. That said, we do urge you to carry the OS maps appropriate to the area. Our maps, of necessity, only cover a narrow band; the OS maps – especially the 1:25,000 series – will give you the full picture and, of course, allow you to deviate safely from the published route should you so wish. Also, you will be able to identify points of interest not available on the guide maps.

The spelling of place names in the text is that shown on OS, but inevitably local variations will occur. For the more hilly walks, we have included height profile diagrams showing the approximate altitude along the route. These may help you to plan your walk more effectively.

During the stalking season (usually September/October, but also at other times) some routes may be closed (see Appendix III Public Rights of Way). In this event, notices may be displayed giving advice on alternative routes, or suggesting that you contact the estate office. It's worth remembering that stalking seldom takes place on a Sunday.

On our research trips we used a GPS (Global Positioning System) navigator as an aid to establishing exact locations. In cloud, or any condition where visibility was severely reduced, or even on a bleak, featureless moorland, it proved very effective. If you carry one of these instruments, it is absolutely critical that you review

and thoroughly understand all aspects of the operating instructions. Your instinct, coupled with your map reading and compass work, should tell you roughly where you are at all times. If the navigator appears to tell you something vastly different it is probably due to an error in usage. Remember: check, check and check again.

Do not underestimate the time required to do a walk. You will know your own walking speed and you may be used to applying Naismith's Rule, and perhaps Trantor's Variations, to calculate the time required to walk a particular route. We think that Naismith is too simple and Trantor is too complicated. When walking in the Highlands, our rule of thumb is:

• 3km per hour, plus a half hour for every 5km as measured on the map (for walking, photography, map consultation, brief refreshments and admiring the view). Therefore:
• A 10km walk will take 10/3 + 1hr = 4hr 20min
• A 15km walk will take 15/3 + 1.5hr = 6hr 30min

This Brook and Hinchliffe Rule works out at about 2.3km per hour. Always overestimate the time required. It is better to arrive a little early, than too late in the day when the light might be fading. All distances in the text are as measured on the relevant OS map; real distances will, of course, be greater due to ascents and descents and variations to avoid difficulties and so on.

There are no rights of way shown on OS maps of Scotland (see Appendix

Bridge sign

CAMUS AONGHAIS
CAMASINAS BURN

Grid reference

OS GRID REFERENCE
NM 656 611

III Public Rights of Way). Contrary to popular supposition, rights of way do exist, and are sometimes shown on signs erected by the Scottish Rights of Way and Access Society. Tales about access problems in Scotland abound, but we have never encountered real difficulties.

One final – and useful – point in this section. All road bridges crossing streams or rivers in Ardnamurchan carry signs with the name of the river on one side and the national grid reference number of their location on the reverse.

Be extra careful when walking on or near the seashore. Tide tables are available from TICs and most hotels, inns and guest houses have copies on display. As a lot of walks in this guide start, and sometimes finish, at sea level; you may climb further than if you were conquering a Munro. Ben More, on Mull, is a classic example of this (and is the only Munro in the Scottish Islands).

WEATHER

Make no mistake about it: Mull is one of the wettest places in the British Isles. The mainland can be pretty wet too. Do not assume that it will be fine tomorrow, or the next day, or the next. We have known 14 consecutive days of sunshine in Scotland. On the other hand, we have known 14 consecutive days on which it has rained most of the time. Your chances of getting wet are pretty high. Assume (like us) that it will rain, and look on it as a bonus if it doesn't.

However, going by the statistics, the best time to walk is in April or May. Be aware of the faint possibility of snow on the high tops in April. Avoid July or August because of possible accommodation problems and the likelihood of the dreaded Scottish midges and clegs. September, October and November can be relatively fine, but remember that some routes may be diverted because of stalking activities. It can be beneficial to take note of television and/or radio weather forecasts, and the local ones can turn out to be quite accurate.

Forecasts are usually displayed in the TICs, who will also provide numbers for telephone weather forecasts.

WALKING GROUPS

One of the attractions of Scotland's Far West is its remoteness. You can walk for several days without seeing any other walkers. Generally speaking we like to walk together, or at most in a party of three or four. This way we can move through the countryside with the minimum of disturbance to ground cover and wildlife. You notice much more when you are with only one or two companions. It's also worth remembering that a large group might have difficulties with accommodation.

At the risk of stating the obvious, we would consider it most unwise to attempt some of the more remote walks alone. Even if going out with a companion, it is sensible to let someone know your intended route – and your estimated time of return – or leave a note, but NOT in your car as this invites intruders. In the event of an emergency the rescue services will need an idea of where you might be.

SHOPS

Once away from Tobermory on Mull, or Strontian on the mainland, shops are few and far between apart from the occasional small store. If you are relying on shops for provisions and so

Carn Mòr in cloud (Walk 4: B8073 (Calgary) to Kilninian)

Pass of Scarduish (Walk 15: Blain Circular)

on, forward planning may be required. However, most hotels, guest houses and B&Bs will provide packed lunches.

PAYMENT

In urban areas we all take for granted the use of bankers' credit and debit cards and sometimes forget that these facilities may not be available in all parts of the British Isles. A lot of places in the Highlands have no shop, let alone a bank or cash dispenser. There are banks at Oban, Fort William, and one bank at Tobermory. Bank vans visit some other areas, but forward planning is required to ensure adequate supplies of cash. Most places will accept cheques, supported by a cheque guarantee card.

CELLPHONES

At the time of writing, cellphones on the Vodafone network seem to work well in most parts of Mull and the mainland, although reception problems naturally occur in areas sheltered from the aerial systems. Cellphones on the Orange network worked less well during our research trips.

DEFINITIONS USED

- **Road**: A way that is metalled and intended for normal motor vehicles
- **Lane**: Along which a motor vehicle could be driven with care, but on which a tractor or 4WD vehicle would have no difficulty
- **Track**: Along which walking is easy, even if the surface is rough, but along which a tractor or 4WD vehicle may have difficulties
- **Path**: Along which only walkers could pass (could also be a bridleway)
- **Trod**: A way made by sheep or other animals, useful for walking
- **N, SE and so on**: Approximate bearings

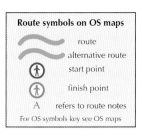

Route symbols on OS maps

route

alternative route

start point

finish point

A refers to route notes

For OS symbols key see OS maps

THE ISLE OF MULL

Raised beach (Walk 5)

Basalt columns on seashore (Walk 15)

'Whatever withdraws us from the power of our senses; whatever makes the past, the distant, or the future, predominate over the present, advances us in the dignity of thinking beings.' **Samuel Johnson**, *A Journey to the Western Isles of Scotland* (1775)

In 1773, Dr Samuel Johnson – writer, critic, lexicographer and conversationalist – had shared a delightful tour of the Hebrides with his friend and biographer James Boswell. If you are looking for peace and quiet with time to advance your thinking and thoroughly relax your senses, rather than experience the hustle and bustle of the tourist routes, we too can heartily recommend a visit to Scotland's Far West, starting with the Isle of Mull.

Mull is an island of many contrasts. Mountains and moors, rocky shores and sandy coves, bare peninsulas and precipitous cliffs, wooded glens and glistening lochs together provide the visitor with an infinite variety of seascapes and landscapes. Even if you're not a geologist, you will find the geology awe-inspiring.

Not to be confused with the Mull of Kintyre (which lies south of the Kintyre peninsula), Mull was known to Ptolemy, the great Egyptian astronomer and geographer, as 'Melaeos'. The meaning of Mull's name has been lost in the passage of time, but some commentators suggest that it may be traced back to mean 'the Mountainous Isle'.

It is the second largest isle of the Inner Hebrides, with an area of nearly 80,000ha, measuring a maximum of 45km from east to west and 40km from south to north. Its 480km coastline is deeply penetrated by sea lochs, especially on the west, and there are some 225km of roadway, varying from short stretches of straight and wide to long stretches of very twisty and very narrow.

GETTING THERE

As with many Scottish islands, Mull's lifelines rely upon the Caledonian MacBrayne ferry services. The most frequent and most used is the 45-minute sailing from Oban on the mainland to Craignure. There is also the 15-minute crossing from Lochaline on the mainland to Fishnish, and the 35-minute less frequent trip from Kilchoan to Tobermory. Other sailings may be arranged with any of several private hire companies. A grass airstrip near Salen may also, by prior arrangement, be used by small aeroplanes.

If you leave the Craignure ferry terminal (overshadowed by the majestic Dun de Ghaoithe ridge) and turn right to head northwards on the A849, you will soon arrive at one of the most delightful small towns in Scotland: Tobermory, the capital of Mull. It takes its name from the Gaelic 'Tobar Mhaire', meaning Mary's Well. Originally developed in 1788 by the British Fisheries Society, Tobermory never really became successful as a fishing village. However, thanks to Calve Island, just a few hundred metres offshore, it has an excellent sheltered harbour with a maritime history going back many hundreds of years.

Oban ferry at Craignure

21

*Concrete seal at
Grass Point*

In 1588 the Spanish galleon *San Juan de Sicilia*, a fugitive of the Armada, dropped anchor in the bay to take on supplies. Legend has it that MacClean of Duart offered provisions in return for the loan of a few hundred troops to assist with the siege of Mingary Castle on the mainland in Ardnamurchan. The siege was unsuccessful, but a rumour had spread that the galleon carried a vast treasure of gold coin. Mysteriously, the ship's magazine exploded and she sank to the seabed about 75m offshore. Since that time nearly 50 diving expeditions have failed to locate the treasure in the wreck, now well and truly buried in the deep harbour mud. Some said the treasure had been taken to Aros Castle, suspiciously close to Duart. But the hoard has not been found.

More recently the harbour became well known to many naval officers and ratings engaged in training for anti-submarine warfare during World War II.

Today the brightly painted waterside buildings nestle in a steep amphitheatre, forming a superb backdrop to one of the finest bays in the Hebrides and attracting boats from far and wide to this popular yachting centre.

As well as hotels, guest houses, inns, cafés, restaurants and B&Bs, there is a bank, museum, post office, TIC, garage and golf course, and a selection of shops. You can walk from the town centre to the lighthouse at Rubha nan Gall (not open to visitors), or enjoy a stroll in Aros Park. Now managed by Forest Enterprise, the park once surrounded a grand Victorian, Scottish baronial mansion, complete with fashionably requisite rhododendrons.

There are maps in the car park giving details of the current network of footpaths.

Tobermory hosts Highland Games in summer, and in October the island's spectacular annual car rally, organised by the Motor and Motorcycle Car Club of Blackburn. The event attracts entries of over 100 cars with many thousands of spectators travelling to the island to watch the thrilling races. Some public roads are closed to enable stages to be run without any speed restriction.

From Tobermory you can travel northwest to Glengorm, with access to wild walking country in the most northerly part of Mull at Ardmore Point. To the west of Tobermory lies Dervaig with its famous Mull Little Theatre, and yet further west is Calgary Bay with a beautiful white sand beach. Some say that emigrants from here founded the city of Calgary in Canada in 1885. North of Calgary is Caliach Point, the most northwesterly part of the island. Turning south down the coast road, with raised beaches nearby, the Isle of Ulva, accessible by a five-minute passenger ferry crossing, will be seen across the water.

Tobermory harbour

*Mull Little Theatre
at Dervaig (Walk 2)*

When you reach the Gruline junction, near the MacQuarie Mausoleum, you are at Mull's narrowest point, a mere 5km from the east coast. Continuing down the west coast will take you around the base of the highest mountain, Ben More (966m). A visit to the summit of the Ben is almost mandatory as the views, on a clear day, are breathtaking. Cutting south across the Ardmeanach Peninsula (with its MacKinnon's Cave, its Wilderness and a demanding walk to the fossil tree) leads you to Loch Scridain and the southern section of the A849. A left turn at the junction will ensure your return to Craignure, but a right turn will take you on the coach-tour route to Iona, with its famous abbey and historical associations with St Columba.

From Iona, your easterly return to Craignure and Tobermory will pass access points to the south coast of the island, leading to such secluded hamlets as Carsaig and Lochbuie. This area is quite different from the rugged north and west coasts. It is gentle, lush and green with, nevertheless, some quite serious walking areas including Carsaig Arches with its soaring cliffs and ramparts of basalt.

Mull has something for everyone. Having visited it once, you are in danger of finding yourself returning time and time again.

THE ISLE OF MULL

IONA

No book on Scotland's Far West would be complete without including a trip to Iona, visited constantly over the last 1500 years or so by pilgrims and others from all round the world.

The island's historical and traditional associations with Columba are well documented. Born a prince, he sailed from Ireland with twelve followers in AD563 at the age of 42. He came to Iona as a self-imposed exile, after a battle over his rights to own and teach from a simple translation of the Bible, recently arrived from the Vatican. He won the battle but, to his horror, this pyrrhic victory cost many, many lives. His missionary instincts prevailing, however, he soon set up a community dedicated to spreading Christianity.

The transition from these simple beginnings to the completion of the grand pink-granite cathedral we see today was by no means easy. The Vikings took against the monastic settlement and razed it to the ground on many occasions between 795 and 986. Time and again the settlement was rebuilt. So important did it become that a mixture of truth and legend lists no less than 48 Kings of Scotland, four Kings of Ireland, eight of Norway, and many Lords of the Isles as having been buried there. More recently the abbey cemetery became the resting place of the late Labour Party leader John Smith, who had been granted special rights to be interred in this most holy place. The abbey became a cathedral in 1500 and much of its 16th-century structure forms the basis of today's well-worked building. Current OS maps show the site as 'St Mary's Abbey'.

The spirit of Columba lives on in Iona. The Reverend George MacLeod, a parish minister in Glasgow, founded the present Iona Community in 1938, dedicated to finding new ways of 'living the gospel'. Today, the community is committed to '. . . rebuilding the common life, through working for social and political change; striving for the renewal of the church with an ecumenical emphasis; and exploring new, more inclusive approaches, to worship, all based on an integrated understanding of spirituality'.

In 1979 Sir Hugh Fraser bought Iona from its long-time owners the Dukes of Argyll, and presented it to the National Trust for Scotland. Now a scheduled ancient monument, the abbey is administered by trustees directed by Historic Scotland.

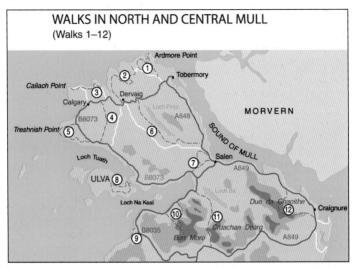

WALKS IN NORTH AND CENTRAL MULL
(Walks 1–12)

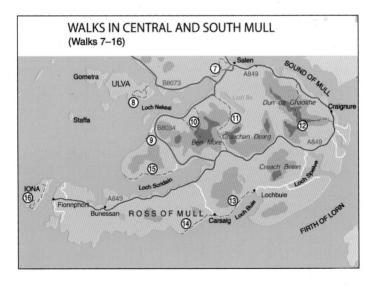

WALKS IN CENTRAL AND SOUTH MULL
(Walks 7–16)

WALK 1

Ardmore Point

Start:	Estate car park Tobermory to Glengorm road (455566)
Finish:	Forest Enterprise car park near the Tobermory to Glengorm road
	(486557)
Distance:	10.5km (6.5 miles)
Route features:	Mostly well-defined forestry tracks and paths, with optional undefined section along rough sea-shore
OS map:	Explorer 374 Isle of Mull North & Tobermory (East Sheet)

During Dr Johnson's travels on Mull in 1773 he was moved to comment that there was little forest area to be seen, and that still seems to be so today. Forest Enterprise owns about 16,000 hectares, around 18 per cent of the total area of the island. The forest at Ardmore is, in the main, mature sitka spruce currently being harvested. When replanting takes place, redesign will ensure more broadleaves to encourage an increase in wildlife and soften the forest boundaries. Please look out for forestry operations during your walk and take note of all written and verbal advice.

To reach the start of the walk, take the Tobermory to Glengorm road westerly and, after about 5km, the estate car park will be seen on the right. The forest is entered after a short walk down a track across a field.

The first part of the walk is through tall trees, but from the clearings you will catch glimpses of the sea and Ardnamurchan. Penalbanach (Pennyland) is the first ruined farm you will see (**E**). The original hamlet of the same name was cleared to create a farm, which was worked until the 1930s before being abandoned.

BLOODY BAY

Before reaching the end of the walk, a little scramble up a steep forest track (**L**) will reveal a superb viewing point high above the waters of Bloody Bay in the Sound. History records that in 1482 the waters of the sea ran red with blood as John McDonald, the last Lord of the Isles, engaged in a fearsome sea battle with his illegitimate son Angus. Many were slaughtered, but Angus was victorious.

Reaching the shore at Ardmore Bay (**F**), listed as a safe temporary anchorage for seagoers, a small hide affords the opportunity for bird and seal watching.

Tide permitting (see **H** in the route notes), a visit to Ardmore Point Light (**I**) is rewarding. Marking the northern entrance of the Sound of Mull, the beam can be seen for 13km. There are uninterrupted views north to Kilchoan on the Ardnamurchan mainland, west to Coll, northwest to Barra and South Uist in the Outer Hebrides, and southeast along the Sound.

Leaving the sea, you will soon arrive at the ruined hamlet of Ardmore (the Large Promontory). As with Penalbanach, this was abandoned in the 1930s. The remains of the school, which had about 30 pupils and presumably served both communities, lie a little further along the forest trail.

Ardmore Light

A short walk will bring you back to another car park near the Glengorm road, about 2km from Tobermory.

Route notes

A   Leave the car park through the gate, to descend on the well-defined track. Keep right at the fork lower down.

B   Enter the forest. The track continues to be well defined. Keep ahead all the way.

C   The track (really a forest road) twists and turns around the gullies and spurs with the occasional view out to sea.

D   The forest road descends gently. At the bend there are fine views N.

E   At the junction, turn left. The remains of Penalbanach are visible on the right. Descend on the track/path.

F   Descend to the shore to visit the bird-/seal-watching hide. Just before the hide, the route continues to the right, on Forestry-made wooden walkways.

G   The going is rough along the edge of the high-water mark.

H   Where the path turns inland you will arrive at a substantial conical-shaped cairn on your left made from sea pebbles. To visit Ardmore Point, leave the main route here and follow the coastline. There is no defined path, only evidence of previous walkers in places. The going is very rough and unsuitable for inexperienced walkers. Some difficulties may be encountered at high tides.

I   From Ardmore Point light you can see Kilchoan in Ardnamurchan and SE along the Sound of Mull. Return to **H** to continue on the defined path SSE.

J   Ascend on the very boggy pathway, passing the remains of Ardmore on your right.

K   Ford the burn and pass more ruins (Ardmore school) on your right.

L   To view the Sound from above Bloody Bay, turn left for 300m or so, then right to ascend a steep track to the ridge. The few metres beyond the ridge to the cliff edge are very difficult, but the view down the Sound is well worth the effort. Return to **L** and continue on the forest road.

M   At the junction, keep left.

N   Continue on the forest road to the Tobermory road.

WALK 2

Glengorm Castle to Dervaig

Start:	Glengorm Castle (441573); visitor car park open 1000–1700
Finish:	Dervaig (432519); no formal car park
Distance:	11km (6.8 miles)
Route features:	Some road walking, forest tracks and paths (sometimes difficult to find)
OS map:	Explorer 374 Isle of Mull North & Tobermory (East Sheet)

As well as being of historical interest, Dervaig, at the head of Loch a' Chumhainn, has been described as Mull's most beautiful village. The church, with its distinctive Irish-style round tower, is near the famous Mull Little Theatre. Would-be theatregoers are advised to book early, as it only seats 43 people. This smallest theatre in the world is due to close at the end of 2005, although new premises are being sought.

To get to the start point, take the Tobermory to Glengorm minor road westerly. A drive of some 8km will bring you to Glengorm Castle, where you can park your vehicle near the coffee shop.

In 1847 James Forsyth became Laird of Quinish and Glengorm. He was not the best-liked of landlords, as he raised rents for no other reason than to increase his personal wealth. Having decided to build a baronial-style house, complete with surrounding rhododendrons, he cleared three crofts to provide an area suitable for his new 'castle'. An old estate woman suggested that Glengorm (meaning 'Blue Glen') would be a name suitable for the residence. This was not a benign proposal as it referred to the days of the Clearances, when the glen was indeed blue from the haze of the fires of burning crofts. The house was completed in 1860, but fate was to take a hand and James Forsyth died before he could take up residence. The

Map continues
p.33

estate was sold in the early 20th century, for its excellent shooting and fishing. Nowadays, as well as sheep and cattle farming, it offers self-catering flats and bed-and-breakfast accommodation. The coffee shop provides snacks and beverages, and has organic food for sale.

The coffee shop also provides a base for a series of short walks on the estate. Walks westerly to Mingary Point, northwesterly to the Bathing Pool, rock pools and nearby Dunara Fort, north-northwesterly to the Flat Rock, and through Ardmore Forest and Bluebell Valley are described in leaflets, with maps, obtainable from the shop. The walks vary in length from about 1.5 to 5km, but you are free to roam at will. Appropriate footwear should be worn, as muddy conditions are likely to be encountered underfoot.

Glengorm Castle

IRON AGE SETTLEMENTS

On the Glengorm Castle–Dervaig walk, after leaving the forest at **F**, you enter an area of Iron Age settlements, a fort at Dun Ban, a fort at Mingary and standing stones at Quinish. As you reach Dervaig, there are yet more sites left by settlers all those 2500 years ago. If time and energy permit, we suggest that you use the many access tracks to deviate and explore some of these sites.

Route notes

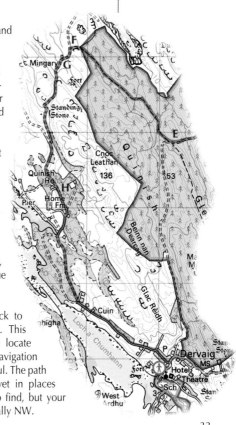

A   Leave the car park and retrace the lane to Sorne.

B   Fork right onto the track and ascend, passing buildings on your left, then enter the wood on a well-defined track.

C   Ignore the track to the right and continue to descend, going left round the bend to reach open ground on your right and the forest on your left. Pass Ballimeanoch.

D   Turn right and, after 400m, enter the forest. Continue on the clear track.

E   At 432548 leave the track to join a path to the right. This point could be tricky to locate and is one where a GPS navigation system would be very useful. The path is variable, being very wet in places and sometimes difficult to find, but your direction should be generally NW.

Glengorm coast

F Leave the forest, turning W then SW to join a track which passes in front of Mingary.

G Leave the precincts of Mingary, passing through a gate to continue on the obvious track.

H The track is well defined. After Home Farm, it becomes a lane that is clear all the way to Dervaig.

WALK 3

Croig to Caliach Point

Start:	Croig (402539); very limited roadside parking
Finish:	Caliach Point (348543); nearest is roadside parking at road head (365537)
Distance:	8km (5 miles)
Route features:	Some road walking with mainly undefined, sometimes rough, walking along coastline
OS map:	Explorer 374 Isle of Mull North & Tobermory (West Sheet)

Cape Wrath is the most northwesterly point of the British mainland, while Caliach Point is the most northwesterly point of Mull. It can be reached by walking along the coast from Croig.

To reach the start, take the B8073 from Tobermory through Dervaig. The minor road to Croig is a right turn (407523) about halfway between Dervaig and Calgary.

There is room to park near Croig's tiny jetty. The Gaelic 'Croig' means 'Cattle Harbour' and it was once used by boats bringing cattle from the Isles of Coll and Tiree. Now only a few local fishermen are to be seen there, and the occasional visitor enjoying a boat trip. A map of 1842 records an inn near the jetty, no doubt well patronised by cattle drovers. Unfortunately there is no sign of the hostelry now.

The way ahead is straightforward until the track fizzles out at **D**. Thereafter it's a case of roughly following the coastline, avoiding most of the ins and outs of the many coves. Away to your left, you will see the occasional dwelling by the roadside, as well as Cillchriosd (Church of Christ).

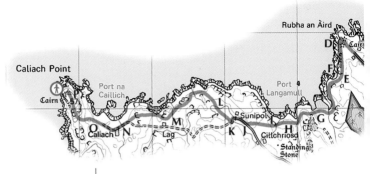

Regaining the road at **J**, you will pass in front of the solitary house at Sunipol (Suni's Farm). There are several local tales about mysterious happenings at this remote spot. One concerns a time when the local minister warned his flock to beware of this place, especially at night. Despite (or because) of this a couple of intrepid souls, perhaps fortified by the odd dram, decided to spend the night there. All went well until the front door suddenly opened as seaweed-covered rocks from the seashore pounded in. One imagines that they left with similar speed and disorder.

Having left the road at **K** and rejoined it at **N**, you will soon reach Caliach, and the road head. You could

ARCHAEOLOGICAL SITES

North of the B8073 road linking Dervaig and Calgary there are many sites of archaeological interest. Bronze Age and Iron Age monuments are to be found in abundance. There are no less than 15 recorded sites, the remains of standing stones, cairns, duns, forts and villages. These may not be apparent to the untrained eye, but serve to remind us that this wild coastal area was once home to a substantial community. There is still much debate about the purpose of standing stones, and it has been suggested that some of the duns and forts may not have been built as defensive positions, but merely to impress the neighbours. A glance at the OS map shows this area to be extensively enclosed, which may be a consequence of these early settlements.

arrange to be picked up from here after visiting the trig point on Caliach Point, a short walk away.

You may wonder why Caliach Point is so called. The name comes from the Gailic 'Cailleach' (Old Woman), referring to a stac, resembling an old woman, which stood at the point until it was destroyed by a severe storm in the late 1950s.

Route notes

A   Proceed ahead on the well-defined track.

B   The right turn in the track is obvious.

C   If you wish, take the grassy track to the right and descend to the shore to visit a pleasant little sandy beach. Otherwise keep ahead on the defined track.

D   The formal track fades out and it is possible to explore the rocky shoreline from here. To continue, take the vague track to the left that degenerates to a faint path. Keep parallel to the shore.

Near Caliach Point

E Bend right on the faint path and descend towards the shore.

F At the shore cross a broken fence and scramble a few feet downwards.

G Follow the shoreline around to the sandy beach.

H Continue to follow the shoreline avoiding the various inlets. The going is fairly rough but straightforward.

I A substantial wall is met, so keep left through the bracken across rough grazing land towards the road.

J Pass through the gate and turn right into the road. Sunipol is on your right.

K Where the road bends left, take the track off to the right towards the shore.

L The track fades out, but keep ahead, descending to more level ground. The labyrinth of paths and cleared ways through the bracken will allow you to follow the shoreline.

M Minor watercourses and rough ground make the going fairly tough.

N When Caliach comes into view, proceed towards the road and approach the dwelling. Pass through the right-hand one of two gates.

O Follow the grassy track to the wall, passing through the left-hand gate. Approach the high ground, ascending and keeping high to the trig point.

P The trig point is the end of the walk. Retrace your steps to the road head.

WALK 4

B8073 (near Calgary) to Kilninian

Start:	Visitor car park on B8073 E of Calgary (395519)
Finish:	Kilninian church (397456); roadside parking
Distance:	7km (4.3 miles)
Route features:	Moorland walking on sometimes undefined wet and boggy paths. Ford(s) to negotiate
OS map:	Explorer 374 Isle of Mull North & Tobermory (West Sheet)

This walk, mainly across moorland, starts near Calgary on the northwest coast of Mull. In the late 19th century emigrants from the area established its Canadian namesake. If you have arranged vehicular support for this walk, your driver may like to spend a relaxing day on the white shell-sand beach of Calgary Bay with its nearby art gallery and nature walk. So pleasant is it that your driver may be inclined to forget to pick you up at Kilninian church at the end of the walk.

B8073 (near Calgary) to Kilninian (Walk 4)

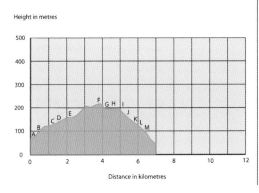

39

To reach the start, take the B8073 from Tobermory. About 2.5km before the hamlet of Calgary a clearly signed car park will be found in the forest on the right.

Nearby, on the other side of the road, a Scottish Rights of Way and Access Society signpost marks the start of the route to Kilninian. Shortly after leaving the forest at **D**, there is a ford which, at the time of our research, was impassable. A scramble up the hill alongside the burn eventually reveals a crossing point, after which you can rejoin the definitive route. Perhaps you will have better luck and be able to cross at the footpath. From here, the route skirting Carn Mòr (343m) originally linked Mornish school and Kilninian. The wet and boggy route across the rather bleak moor is aptly named Crois Mhoraidh Bhubh, the Crossing of Black Mary. The path is ill defined in places, but the highest part at Lochan na h-Earba provides a welcome reference point. From here, it is a gentle descent to the church at Kilninian with pleasant views of the Treshnish Isles and Loch Tuath.

Route notes

A   A gate (397519) gives access to the forest just E of the car park and on the S side of the B8073. A Scottish Rights of Way and Access Society signpost indicates a route to Kilninian. Pass through the gate into the forest and follow the well-defined path.

B   Right and left to continue.

C   Leave the forest.

D   About 150m later there is a ford that may be impassable when the burn is in spate. A crossing point can be found above the waterfall.

E   The path is defined, but boggy in places.

F   Pass Lochan na h-Earba on your left about 50m away and start to descend on the fairly well-defined path.

G Some 200m past the lochan, the path seems to disappear into a shallow gully. At this point, fork left to cross the watercourse and join the fairly well-defined old track which is boggy in places.

H The track skirts around a large, boggy, level hollow.

I On leaving the hollow and starting to descend, the path is defined with a line of rocks on your left.

J Path well defined.

K Pass through the gate which joins a wire fence with a drystone wall.

L About 100m after the gate, a double footpath appears in the bracken. Do NOT take this, but take the right fork into the bracken on a narrow path that becomes clearer lower down.

M The path approaches a house with a caravan. At this point, fork right to pass in front of these. Use the access track, passing through the gate, to descend to the road at Kilninian church.

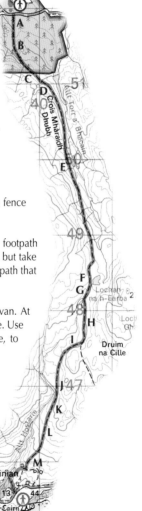

Burn in spate

KILNINIAN CHURCH

The date above the door of Kilninian church implies that it was built in 1755, but it was actually rebuilt that year. There has been a church here since the 16th century, and very probably before that. It is thought that the name Kilninian, pronounced 'Kilnnan', has nothing to do with St Ninian. The most likely, rather charming, derivation is from the Gaelic Cill Naoi Nighean, the Church of the Nine Maidens. It really is worthwhile spending a few minutes in the church, with its unusual benches and several examples of ornately carved 16th-century gravestones in the vestry at the back. Sadly it is not known whom the gravestones remember, as their names have been lost with the passage of time.

Kilninian church with cross

WALK 5

Treshnish Headland

Start:	Car park on B8073 S of Calgary (361485) in roadside disused quarry
Finish:	B8073 NW of Kilninian (577464); parking in roadside excavation
Distance:	9km (5.5 miles)
Route features:	Tracks, defined paths and some undefined moorland walking
OS map:	Explorer 374 Isle of Mull North & Tobermory (West Sheet)

This walk is, in our view, one of the most impressive on Mull. The raised beaches, brought about by a combination of sea-moulded tertiary lava flow and isostosy (the earth rising due to melting of the ice following the last ice age), provides a superb walking platform about 45m above sea level. The rugged coastline below has several caves, stacs and arches to explore. The Treshnish Isles, about 4km out to sea, are of volcanic origin and can be clearly seen during the walk. All are now uninhabited apart from breeding seals and seabirds. Lunga is the largest and Bac Mór, commonly referred to as the Dutchman's Cap because of its shape, is visible beyond Lunga.

House at Treshnish with Buddhist flags and rainbow

Gate en route and Treshnish Isles

The B8073 road loops from Tobermory through Dervaig and Calgary, then turns south and southeast towards Kilninian. About 2.5km beyond Calgary Bay a car park in a quarry is shown on the OS map. Walk north from here for about 250m to join a track off to the left towards Treshnish Cottages.

The hamlet at Haunn (**C**) is somewhat unusual in that the cottages, once belonging to a family of fishermen, are not deserted piles of rubble but neat and tidy holiday homes. Having reached the sea cliffs around **D**, there are many opportunities, tides permitting, for the more adventurous to descend to the rocky foreshore. It is not surprising that this photogenic area was used for location shooting by the producers of *The Eye of the Needle*. The way along the raised beach is superb walking and even has evidence of duns and forts for those interested in matters archaeological.

The definitive route turns left at **I** – where there are the ruins of a medieval chapel – to ascend a barely visible zigzagging one-time pony track to the deserted village of Crackaig. This victim of the Clearances used to be home to a community of 200 or so. One should pause to

45

WHISKY STILL

When you arrive at I, turn right down a steep gully to the rocky shore and right again to find the opening to the 'still' cave, containing the remnants of the 4.5m-wide foundations of a large still. Though disused since the mid 18th century, the whisky it produced retains its reputation for good quality.

admire the skills and workmanship of those who shaped the rounded corners of the stones to make the tiny buildings more storm-resistant.

From Crackaig, the undefined route goes right up the hillside to find a contour around Beinn Reudle (232m). A descent to a watercourse reveals the cottage at Reudle. It is interesting to note that the cottage has got a modern first floor, built on top of a restored original ground floor. An easy walk along a clearly defined track returns you to the B8073.

Deserted village of Crackaig

Route notes

A   Leave the B8073 on the track leading to the trees.

B   At the cottages and farm buildings, keep left to pass on the S side of a substantial barn. Continue on the well-defined track.

C   At Haunn pass in front of the cottages and through the gate into the field. The track is less defined but still clear.

D   The track, cut from the rock face, degenerates to a path and descends to the raised beach.

E   The way is less clear, but keep high on the raised beach.

F   A defined path is easy to follow on the raised beach.

G   Keep to the path which is still clear, but more convoluted.

H   The path remains clear and wends its way amongst the rocks.

I   On reaching a waterfall high in the gully on your left, proceed ahead on the path around the spur to arrive at the remains of old walls. Now ascend left to leave the raised beach. A zigzag path becomes discernible. If you miss this left turn and ascent, you will soon realise your mistake as the path ahead becomes impassable.

J   When the path levels out, the remains of houses at Crackaig are visible to your left. Now turn right to leave the path and ascend the hill ahead (no obvious path through heather and bracken). Keep S of E on the contour.

K   Turn E and keep on the contour as far as possible amongst the hillocks.

L   Turn N of E, again on the contour as far as possible.

M   Descend to the watercourse and make for the cottage at Reudle. A path is discernible on the approach to the cottage. About 50m before the cottage, bear left to cross the burn and join the green lane which then bends right, changing to a gravel surface.

N   Follow the track all the way to the B8073.

WALK 6

Torr to Aros

Start:	Torr, S of Loch an Torr on B8073 Tobermory to Dervaig road (451522); roadside parking
Finish:	Forest Enterprise car park (551454)
Distance:	14.5km (9 miles)
Route features:	Tracks and defined paths; sometimes very wet in forest area
OS map:	Explorer 374 Isle of Mull North & Tobermory (East Sheet)

This walk takes you along the western side of Loch Frisa, the largest loch on Mull. The going is generally easy apart from one or two very wet bits in the forest (**C**).

Take the B8073 road from Tobermory to Dervaig. About 7.5km out of Tobermory, just past Loch an Torr, there is space to park near a new bridge at 451523. Walk a few metres ahead towards Dervaig and turn left into a track at the bend in the road.

There may be occasional glimpses of the loch from the forest and you may even see its two tiny islands, Eilean Bàn and Eilean Dubh (Fair Island and Black Island). There is evidence to suggest that a crannog had been built on Eilean Bàn, and why anyone should want to build a fortified timber dwelling on such a small island is an intriguing question. Across the loch is the highest hill on north Mull, Speinne Mor (444m).

The remnants of standing stones at **I** are marked on the OS map with the Gaelic 'Carrachan', as well as with the English translation.

After negotiating the sheep pens at Tenga, you will soon arrive at the Ledmore river. If you want to try your luck on the stepping-stones, you will find them upriver from the bridge at **M**.

AROS CASTLE

Aros Castle was built in the 13th century by the MacDougals as part of the coastal defensive system. The ruins stand on the edge of a small crag on the Aros river estuary, north of Salen Bay. It is difficult to imagine that the remnants of walls and piles of rubble once formed the principal seat of the MacDonalds, Lords of the Isles in the 15th century. Last inhabited in 1608, the castle was left to disintegrate after guarding the northern approaches to the bay for 300 years.

At **N**, you have the option of returning to your starting point near Loch an Torr. To do this proceed ahead until you reach a forest road, at which turn left. This will take you past Lettermore Farm and along the east side of the loch. Note that we have not researched this alternative.

The **definitive route** goes through the forest and ends at the Forest Enterprise car park.

Wet map drying out (not entirely uncommon on Mull)

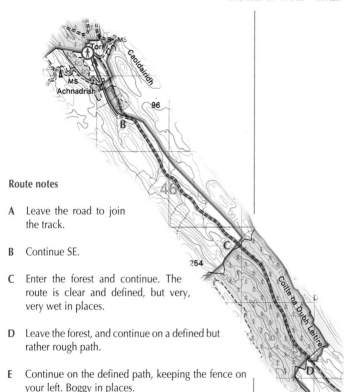

Route notes

A Leave the road to join the track.

B Continue SE.

C Enter the forest and continue. The route is clear and defined, but very, very wet in places.

D Leave the forest, and continue on a defined but rather rough path.

E Continue on the defined path, keeping the fence on your left. Boggy in places.

F At the corner of the fence, by the gate, continue ahead, descending slightly. The path crosses the watercourse on a sleeper, presumably a footbridge in earlier times. Follow the defined path along the contour.

G The path descends towards a defined track.

H Join the track, which then ascends gently. The way fades out over rough grazing but keep S of E to reach a gate.

Map continues p.52

I   There are standing stones away to the right. Pass through the gate, now keeping SE. Then descend to the track where it is cut from the bank. Make for the gate in the fence, which is clearly visible.

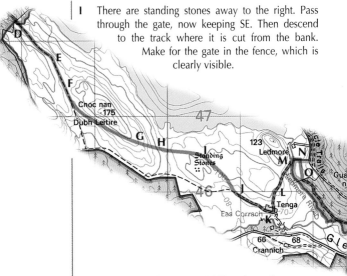

J   Pass through the gate and follow the well-defined track to Tenga.

K   At Tenga, pass through the three gates of the sheep pens and then turn left up the track before the house. Ascend to pass through the gate.

L   Continue, then start to descend to another gate at which you can see a footbridge in trees by the river. Keep ahead, following the electricity pylons aiming for the bridge. Don't be tempted to follow the apparent route to the left.

M   Keep right, descending to cross the footbridge. Then ascend into the field, keeping the fence on your left.

N   On reaching a gate on your left, turn right and cross the field path to the forest.

O   Enter the forest through the gate and continue ahead
      on the forest road for 3km to the forest exit at:

P   Here is a picnic site and car park.

WALK 7

Mull Coast to Coast

Start:	Killiechronan (540412); roadside space near entrance to track leading to Killiechronan Farm (569434)
Finish:	Salen (570432); roadside parking near old jetty beside A849
Alternative start:	On A489 just N of Salen (569434) near old jetty
Alternative finish:	Salen (570432) or Killiechronan (540412)
Distance:	6km (3.7 miles)
Route features:	Tracks and well-defined, but sometimes wet and boggy, paths
OS map:	Explorer 374 Isle of Mull North & Tobermory (East Sheet)

Having walked Wainwright's 306km Coast to Coast across England many years ago and, more recently, having written our 309km Alternative Coast to Coast, it seemed natural to do the Mull Coast to Coast, a distance of only 4km as the crow flies. We offer a route from Killiechronan to Salen direct, and an alternative from Salen via Glenaros House to Killiechronan. You can, of course, combine the two to make a circular walk from Salen.

To start from Killiechronan, drive north from Craignure to Salen and turn left to take the B8035 for about 4km. Turn right at the junction to join the B8703 for a further 1km to arrive at Killiechronan, where you can park on the right-hand side of the road at the entrance between Killiechronan House and a sawmill.

At **C**, there is access to view the (unnamed) lochan. Point E marks the summit of the walk, at 100m; looking back you can see Loch na Keal (variously translated as Loch of the Narrows or Loch of the Churches, and known as Loch Scaffort until 1790). Ahead is the Sound of Mull, with a backdrop formed by the hills of Morvern.

STAFFA AND FINGAL'S CAVE

The isthmus between Salen and Killiechronan is so narrow that in the early 1800s, about the time of the composer Mendelssohn's visit, passengers for the Isle of Staffa and Fingal's Cave crossed from the mainland to Aros. From there they took horse transport to Killiechronan to re-embark for the final stage of the journey to the isle made immortal by the music of the *Hebrides Overture*.

To start from Salen, park off-road near the jetty on the A849 just north of the village. Join the route through a gate on the left at 569434.

After **D1**, ford the Alt a' Choisteil and ahead on the skyline is a ruined fort, Cnoc na Sroine. If you visit this site you will discover a few thousand tonnes of rock rubble with one or two remnants of walls. The all-round views from this vantage point are worth the effort involved in getting there.

When you arrive at **G1**, turn left to return to Salen or right for Killiechronan.

Route notes:
Killiechronan to Salen

A   Leave the B8073 at 540412, to ascend the track between

the drive to Killiechronan House and a sawmill. About 100m from the road, turn sharp right on the track leading to a gate. Pass through the gate and follow the well-defined, well-made, track.

B   Where the track bifurcates, take the right fork to pass through the gate into the forest. Continue on the well-defined forest track.

C   Above the lochan, turn left following the defined path which is wet and boggy in places.

D   Pass through a gate between fences for a few metres and through another gate to leave the forest. Continue on the wet, boggy, convoluted but well-defined path.

E   At the summit both the Sound of Mull and Loch na Keal are visible. The path is still defined, wet and boggy.

F   Enter open, natural woodland, descending on the path to join the A849 at Salen beside a substantial house (once a church) set above the road.

Route notes: Salen to Killiechronan

A1   About 0.5km from Salen going northwards on the A849 is an old jetty on the right. About 100m beyond this, on the left, gates give access to a well-defined track through the woods.

B1   On leaving the woods, the track continues through fields, passing through gates to reach the precincts of Glenaros House.

C1   Pass the house (100m to your right) and through the gate (or use the dilapidated stile). Continue towards the cottage, leaving this enclosure through another gate into the access track. Keep to the right of Kate's Cottage and pass through yet another gate to the

THE ISLE OF MULL – WALK 7

tracks beyond. Take the left fork, which ascends with a wall on your left.

D1 Follow the defined track, albeit wet in places.

E1 At the summit of Cnoc na Sroine there is a prehistoric fort to your left. The way is very boggy at this point.

F1 On the descent, the path is defined

G1 Join the original route and either continue, right, into the forest and down to Killiechronan, or turn left to go back to Salen.

Note: that the section between **F1** and **G1** is NOT that shown on OS.

Walks in central Mull based on Craignure

WALK 8

Ulva

Start & finish:	Ulva ferry (446399); car park approx 100m before ferry
Distance:	8.5km (5.3 miles)
Route features:	Well-defined tracks and paths, mainly waymarked by white stones and signs
OS map:	Explorer 374 Isle of Mull North & Tobermory (East Sheet)

We make no excuses for including another island (as well as Iona – see p100) in this section of walks on Mull. Ulva, separated from the mainland by a 300m-wide sound, is a delightful place – and one we suspect you will wish to visit more than once.

ULVA

Ulva is only small, measuring 7km by 3km. It has a satellite island, Gometra, a mere 3km by 2km and joined by a bridge to its western end. The owners of Ulva have signposted several walks, the routes being defined by white-topped posts and white-painted rocks, but you are free to roam where you will and without fear of traffic as there are no surfaced roads on the island. You may, however, meet the occasional farm vehicle. Of the 'official walks' we have chosen the one we think is the best.

Owned by the Clan MacQuarie for many generations, the island of Ulva was sold in 1777 when the chief fell on hard times and had to raise money to pay off his debts. In 1785 Ulva was bought by the Macdonalds, pioneers in the kelp industry, and it is said that the laird became rich and the island more populated. In 1835 the island was

Basalt columns on Ulva coast

sold to a notoriously wicked laird, Francis William Clark. This purchase was a harbinger of hard times for his tenants.

In the early 1800s the population led a life of relative contentment. Each family had at least one boat and the cultivation of potatoes, the local staple diet, was so successful that the excesses were exported to the mainland. By 1837 there were 600 people living in 16 hamlets, supported by all the artisans necessary to a thriving community. Clark boasted about the success of his investment, and the Statistical Account of 1845 describes the effective growing of wheat and beans. Then disaster struck.

The kelp market collapsed. At the same time, potato blight destroyed the crop and, as in many parts of Scotland, crofting was out and sheep were in. The destruction of the traditional way of life of the highlands and islands – the Clearances – is well documented, and it appears that Clark was one of its most ruthless lairds. Between 1846 and 1851 he almost decimated the population, driving his factor to fire the roofs of the crofts and evict the tenants. By 1881, only 53 people remained. These, poor souls, were forced to live at Desolation Point on the northeast coast, not even allowed to build

Ferry sign at Ulva

permanent accommodation. Clark's regime resulted in the island's population consisting of sheep, with a mere handful of estate workers in attendance.

The Clark family owned Ulva until 1945, when it was sold to Lady Congleton. Her daughter, Jean Howard, now owns the island, with her son, Jamie Howard, as estate manager.

To get to the starting point of the walk, drive north from Craignure to Salen and take the B8035, turning right to join the B8073 after about 4km. A further 10km or so will bring you to the left (signed) turn leading to the Ulva ferry car park. Just 3km up the road from this left turn are the famous Eas Fors waterfalls. The name is tautological – both words mean waterfall – but they are certainly worth a visit and there is a car park nearby.

On landing at the island, you will be faced by the Boathouse (**A**), which is a visitor centre, gift shop and café. Here you can view the interpretive display, purchase gifts and guidebooks, have a snack and even enjoy a plate of the oysters for which Ulva is famed. There are also toilets and a public telephone in an old red telephone box. Be warned, however, that if you want to use the 'phone in the tomato-growing season you will

FERRY TO ULVA

The on-demand passenger ferry crossing to Ulva takes only four or five minutes and the method of summoning the ferry is easy and clearly explained. It runs from 0900 to 1700 Monday to Friday; is always closed on Saturdays, but open on Sundays between June and September. The telephone number for enquiries is 06885 500 226, and the estate office is on 06885 500 264.

have to wedge yourself in the box alongside a couple of tomato plants. The Boathouse was built in 1989 on the site of an old temperance inn, which burnt down in 1880 and lay in ruins for years.

Ulva House (**C**) is also relatively modern, having been built in the early 1950s on the site of 19th-century Ulva House, which burnt down whilst being restored and modernised.

When you get down to the southern coastal cliffs (**H**, **I** & **J**), do not miss the basalt columns. Neither as big nor as magnificent as those on Staffa, these examples of basalt lava polygonal columns are, nevertheless, striking.

Between **K** and **L** you will see the 'lazy beds', used for cultivating potatoes in the 18th and early 19th centuries. Here the route passes near a cave in crags on the right, where the grandparents of the famous Scottish missionary and traveller, David Livingstone, were reputed once to have lived. They are also supposed to have lived in a croft, now known as Livingstone's Cabin (**L**).

Prominent on a nearby conical hilltop, on the site of an old fort (Dun Bhiormuil) is the Clark Memorial, where many of the family are buried. If you venture to explore you will find that there is no gate in the high surrounding wall.

On reaching the viewpoint at **O**, you can continue walking to inspect the derelict hamlets of Ormaig and Cragaig, both victims of the Clearances. Upon returning to **O**, your return route to the ferry passes the island's small reservoir and within sight of the church and manse. If you are intent on exploring Gometra, this is best accessed via the track running along the north flank of Ulva. Remember that the last ferry leaves at 1700.

Route notes

A Leave the ferry and turn right in front of the Boathouse, then left following the well-defined track.

B Turn left at the finger-post to follow the track to Ulva House.

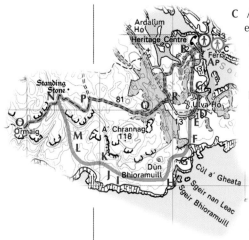

C At the white gate (an entrance to the house), turn left with the track and follow it around the grounds.

D Keep ahead at the finger-post, following the track round to the right and then to the left.

E At the farm (Meall Min), turn left at the finger-post and descend the straight track towards the sea.

F Pass through the gate in the deer fence and continue on the track. After a few metres the track becomes a path.

G The path divides at a point some 10m before a fence. The more defined path bends right. However, take the lesser path to the left, which passes on the sea-ward side of a fence. White-painted stones define the way.

H The path is fairly well defined, marked by white stones.

I Keep on the marked path, parallel to the cliff on open ground.

J The path becomes rough in sparse woodland, with ambiguous side paths. Make sure you follow the white marker stones. If you lose sight of the stones, reverse until you find them.

K   Cross through bracken on open ground, the path being marked by white-topped posts. Turn with the path to approach the ruins of Livingstone's Cabin, with its large white plaque (unfortunately illegible at the time of research).

L   Leave the ruin, to follow the markers leading northwards away from the coast.

M   Enter woodland, climbing.

N   At the bealach, a well-defined track is joined, with a standing stone (recently re-erected in an upright position) in a field some 200m below. Turn left and follow the track to the viewpoint at:

O   Continue on the track as far as you wish. Return on the track to N and carry on walking.

P   At the finger-post, turn right to descend into woodland at:

Q   The track is well defined and passes through a gate in a deer fence.

R   At the T-junction (finger-post), turn left. Follow the descending track back to the ferry.

WALK 9

Mackinnon's Cave

Start & finish:	Visitor car park at Balmeanach Farm off B8035 (448331)
Distance:	3km (1.9 miles) return
Route features:	Tracks and paths, sometimes partly defined, wet in places; scramble over rough sea-shore
OS map:	Explorer 375 Isle of Mull East (West Sheet)

The longest measurable stretch of land from north to south in Scotland is Cape Wrath to the Mull of Galloway, a distance of 441km. The greatest breadth is from Applecross to Buchan Ness, 248km. In many cases, numerous arms of the sea penetrate so far inland that salt water is seldom more than 65km away. It has been estimated that the length of the coastline is 3700km. In Scotland's Far West, the shores of the mainland and the islands are particularly rugged, with many beaches, stacs, coves, cliffs and, especially, caves. At 30m high, the biggest cave in the Hebrides is said to be Mackinnon's Cave on Mull.

Situated on the uninhabited Isle of Staffa, Fingal's Cave is probably the best-known cave in the United Kingdom. Visited by thousands of people every year, it was made famous by the composer Felix Mendelssohn. Already a well-known writer of romantic music at the age of 20, he was also one of the first composers to write concert overtures. His *Die Fingalshöle*, or *Hebrides Overture*, written shortly after his visit to Staffa in 1829, brought him even greater acclaim and had a big impact on European music. After hearing his overture, people from all walks of life flocked to see what had inspired its creation. Artists, explorers, poets, writers and even Queen Victoria and Prince Albert made the pilgrimage to Staffa. Wordsworth, visiting in 1833, was so disgusted with the

large crowds clamouring to visit the cave that he was
moved to write:

> *We saw, but surely in the motley crowd*
> *Not one of us has felt, the far-famed sight;*
> *How could we feel it? Each the others blight,*
> *Hurried and hurrying volatile and loud.*

The cave, set in 41m-high cliffs, is the biggest on
Staffa, 20m high and 74m deep. It is named after the leg-
endary Irish hero Fionn MacCool, (in Gaelic 'Fionn na
Ghal'), who defended the Hebrides from Viking raiders
in the 3rd century. It is not known whether he actually
visited the cave itself.

A visit to Mackinnon's Cave should be much less
frustrating than Wordsworth's experience on Staffa.
When Johnson and Boswell came to inspect it in 1773,
they measured the depth with a walking stick, surpris-
ingly accurately. They found it to be 151m, nearly twice
as long as Fingal's Cave and much longer, wider and
higher than Macdonald's or St Francis' Caves on Eigg –
indeed, the biggest cave in the Hebrides.

To visit the cave – only accessible at low tide – first
consult the tide tables available from TICs and usually on
display in inns, guest houses and hotels on Mull. Drive
from Craignure on the A849 towards Fionnphort and
after 25km turn right to join the B8035 towards Gribun.
On descending a hill towards the sea and Gribun Cliffs,
turn left into the Balmeanach Farm access lane, signed

THE NAMING OF MACKINNON'S CAVE

As is often the case, there are at least two accounts of how Mackinnon's
Cave on Mull got its name. Some say it was named after Abbot Mackinnon
from Iona, who made it his personal sanctuary. Others say that the local
people, wanting to know the depth of the cave, sent in Piper Mackinnon
with his dog. Deep inside he was confronted by a witch (or fairies?) who
made him continue playing until he ran out of breath and died. His – now
hairless – dog returned to the cave mouth alone, and Mackinnon was never
seen again.

Mackinnon's Cave. There is a public car park on the right just before the farm gates. You can also drive via Salen on the B8035, approaching Gribun and the farm entrance from the north.

The short walk to the cave is not difficult and, assuming the tide is well out, once on the shingle a scramble over large, sometimes slippery, rocks will bring you to the cave entrance. If you enter the cave, with its pebble floor at the entrance and sand in the main chamber, make sure your torch and spare batteries are in good order. Also, beware of the fairies.

Route notes

A   Leave the car park and walk S towards the farm. Walk ahead to pass the house on your left and on through the gate. Bend left to pass farm buildings on your right.

B   Pass through another gate near the farm buildings and continue on the track. Turn right with the track, keeping the fence on your right. Leave the track where it bends sharp left. Join the path ahead, keeping the fence on your right.

C   Continue on the partly defined path, which is boggy in parts, still with the fence on your right.

D   Pass through the gate to descend to the shoreline and continue ahead on the shingle.

E   Beyond the flotsam and jetsam (wood, rope and plastics), leave the shoreline to ascend the grassy cliff to locate a very narrow path which is somewhat precarious in parts.

F   The grassy path ends just before the waterfall, leaving a scramble over rocks to reach the cave mouth. The cave is only accessible at low tide.

Return by the same route.

WALK 10

Ben More

Start & finish:	Roadside parking on B8035 shores of Loch na Keal (493360)
Alternative finish:	B8035 1.5km from parking area (407367)
Distance:	9.5km (6 miles)
Route features:	Tracks and paths, sometimes partly defined. Optional pathless, steep, sometimes very wet and boggy, descent
OS map:	Explorer 375 Isle of Mull East (West Sheet)

The name Ben More (meaning 'Big Mountain') is quite appropriate, as it can be seen from many parts of the island. Often with an Everest-like plume of cloud from its summit, the Ben and its surrounding peaks and ridges form a magnificent backcloth on the eastern approaches.

The road from Salen to Loch na Keal, across the narrowest part of the island, divides Mull into two quite

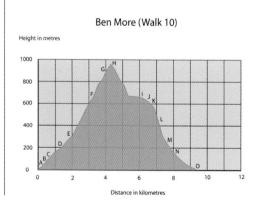

Ben More (Walk 10)

distinct geological areas. The north is a landscape of
trap-rock plateaux, formed millions of years ago by the
successive cooling of layers of lava. To the south, in con-
trast, there are the remains of two enormous calderas,
which have been sculptured by the ever-changing weath-
ers of countless years. To their west stands Ben More;
at 967m the highest mountain on Mull. As Skye is now
linked to the mainland by the Kyle of Lochalsh–Kyleakin

*Ben More across
Loch na Keal*

ALTERNATIVE DESCENT FROM BEN MOR

The quickest and easiest way down is to retrace your steps. However, we
offer an alternative descent from **F**. This route is quite delightful, though the
descent at **K** is very steep in places and the ground at **M**, followed by the wet
path at **N**, can be very boggy and wet.

On arrival at the road, your vehicle should be 1.5km away to the left.

Walkers on Ben More

bridge, and so technically is not an island, Ben More, at 3171ft, is the only Munro in the Scottish Isles.

As with most well-known mountains, there is a multitude of ways to the summit, and we have chosen the classic route. This is perhaps the easiest ascent, but extra brownie points may be claimed as it starts from sea level.

To reach the starting point, drive north from Craignure to Salen and take the B8035. After about 12km there is usually plenty of parking space on the loch side of the road. The Isle of Eorsa should be easily visible across the water.

The first part of the ascent (**A–D**) is quite gentle, but can be boggy in parts. Keep looking back at the views which get better the higher you go. To the northwest the Isle of Ulva should be visible, with the distinctive profiles of the Treshnish Isles in the background.

At about 600m, the 'big mountain' starts to live up to its name. The way up the spur (**E**) and the rocky buttress (**F**) is marked by several cairns. However, the apparent summit ahead is false. Only on reaching **G** is the real summit a relatively flat stroll away across a few hundred metres of well-defined rocky path.

There is a rudimentary stone shelter at the summit cairn, often full of early-bird walkers enjoying a well-earned snack. On clear days the views are immense, extending from the Hebrides to Ireland in the west, whilst to the northeast the Ben Nevis massif is apparent in all its glory.

Route notes

A   At 493360 on the B8035, leave the road up the track leading to Dhiseig.

B   Keep the cottage on your left and ascend the defined path.

C   Cross a fence and continue ascending the moor on the defined path. There is a labyrinth of paths, but you may like to choose the one that keeps you within sound and often sight of the burn (Abhainn Dhiseig).

D   Keep beside the burn and then cross it.

From Ben More towards Ulva

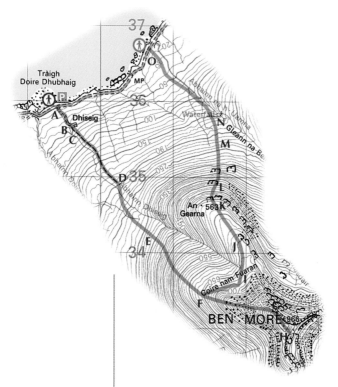

E Where the ground becomes steeper and less boggy, diverge from the burn to ascend the spur. An occasional cairn guides the way.

F On arriving at the rocky buttress, the path becomes clear with many cairns to guide the way. Make for the clearly visible but false summit.

G The way levels out, the main summit being a few hundred metres further on at a tumbledown stone shelter and cairn

H   There are several routes off the summit, the easiest being to retrace your steps.

For the alternative return route, retrace your steps from the summit to **F** and leave the route eastwards. No path.

I   Turn NE then N to access the ridge of An Gearna.

J   Pass the lochans, heading NNW.

K   Start the steep descent. There is no path and care must be taken amongst the rocky outcrops.

L   Keep descending northwards.

M   The ground becomes less steep, but very rough and boggy.

N   Join a very wet path descending NW beside the Abhainn na h-Uamha.

O   The path leads to the B8035 where the burn enters the sea.

WALK 11

Loch Ba to Glen More

Start:	Estate entrance at Knock, on B8035 between Loch na Keal and Loch Ba (545388)
Finish:	Old road just off A849 in Glen More (564306)
Distance:	10.5km (6.5 miles)
Route features:	Tracks and fairly well-defined paths, wet in places; river to cross; optional pathless rough descent
OS map:	Explorer 375 Isle of Mull East (West Sheet)

Geologists are of the opinion that the area around Loch Ba, Glen Cannel and Glen Clachaig is the textbook example of glaciation in Mull.

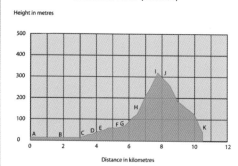

Loch Ba to A849 (Walk 11)

About 50 million years ago a huge volcanic complex developed at the head of what is now Loch Ba. Pressure built up to such an extent that the volcano exploded with intense fury and its central dome collapsed, leaving a ring dyke more than 20km in diameter.

MACQUARIE'S MAUSOLEUM

If you are interested in matters Australian, you may wish to visit MacQuarie's Mausoleum on your way to the starting point. Born in 1761 on the Isle of Ulva, and after distinguished service in the Black Watch, Major General Lachlan MacQuarie was appointed Governor of New South Wales in 1810. The colony, mostly populated by convicts, was in a desperate state, suffering from deprivations caused by monopolists and land developers. MacQuarie took control of the situation and, by dint of sheer hard work and perseverance, created a state of prosperity to be enjoyed by all. In 1821 'The Father of Australia', as he came to be known, returned to Britain, bought the Salen estate and created the village within it. He died in 1824 at his Gruline house, where the nearby mausoleum houses his remains together with those of several members of his family. He is commemorated in Australia by having a harbour, an island, a lake, a pass, a plain, a port and a town, as well as many roads, named after him, and his name crops up all over the place. He was also responsible for building the Great Western Highway through the Blue Mountains.

The comings and goings of later ice ages smoothed the rocks and shaped the valleys. At the mouths of the glens there are many erratics (ice-borne rocks) as well as many drumlins (glacial deposits of boulder clays). Over millennia, the drumlins have been shaped into smooth, elongated mounds, which can be seen very clearly on the eastern slopes of Glen Clachaig.

MacQuarie's Mausoleum

More recently, during the 18th and early 19th centuries, cattle drovers used the valley as a route from Knock into Glen More. The luxurious grazing in the glen was woven into the system of fattening up livestock on the way to mainland markets, using Grass Point, near Craignure, as an embarkation point.

To reach the starting point of the walk, drive north from Craignure to Salen and take the B8035. After about 4km you will arrive at a road junction. Keep ahead, passing a sign to MacQuarie's Mausoleum on the left. Pass over a narrow, hump-backed bridge (built to span the River Ba at the time of the Clearances) and you will soon arrive at a very sharp right bend in the road at Knock. Turn left on this bend to enter the estate entrance where there is room to park. If you are here in the stalking season (August to October) there is a sign at the gates giving information; phone 01680 300358 or 01680 300380.

Having joined the estate road (**A**), you will soon pass Benmore Lodge sheltering in the trees on your left at the edge of the loch. At **C**, about halfway up the Loch, the drove road bifurcates. The sign giving directions to Glen Connel and Glen Clachaig had been 'removed' at the time of our visit. However, take the right fork and eventually cross the burn on the new bridge near Clachaig. Further along, when you get down to the River Clachaig, it is important to locate the small cairn on a grassy river bank near to the water, as this marks the crossing point. It may be necessary to wade if the river is in spate. From

Loch Ba

Near Loch Ba

this point, the bealach at Carn Cul Righ Albainn, with Cruachan Dearg (704m) to its left and the conical A' Chioch (867m) to its right dominate the head of the valley.

The path up the side of the glen is fairly well defined, with occasional stones marking the edge of the old drove road. Several paths converge at the bealach. From here it is also possible to get to the top of Ben More, via a difficult westerly rocky ridge beyond the summit of A' Chioch. The bealach is known as 'The Cairn with its Back to Scotland', so called because it was supposed to have once marked the boundary between the Picts and the Scots.

From the bealach our definitive route takes the well-defined path, wet in places, south-southeasterly down the east side of Allt Teanga Brideig to the bridge at Teanga Brideig on the old road near the A849 in Glen More.

ALTERNATIVE DESCENT TO GLEN MORE

Not for the weary or inexperienced walker – another well-defined path goes south-southwest from the bealach down the west side of Allt Teanga Brideig. Although OS Explorer maps show the path going all the way to Ardvergnish, near the B8035, it disappears on the ground after about 1km. Continue southwesterly over the broad ridge. Turning south (away from the OS route) when you see Loch Scridain enables you to make a steep descent to 553304 on the A849 in Glen More. You will now be about 1.5km west of the bridge at Teanga Brideig. It's very rough going and pathless, but presents fine views over the loch.

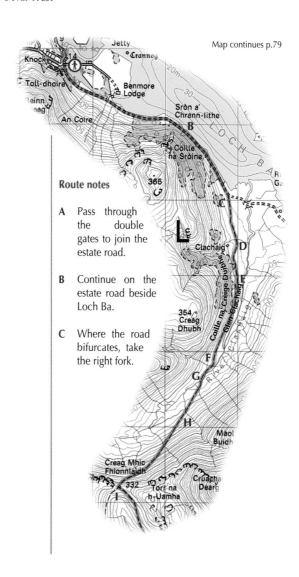

Map continues p.79

Route notes

A   Pass through the double gates to join the estate road.

B   Continue on the estate road beside Loch Ba.

C   Where the road bifurcates, take the right fork.

D Where the road turns sharp right to approach the ruins of Clachaig, keep ahead on the grassy track.

E The way is well defined, but varies between path and track status. Very wet in places.

F At about 566350, the track disappears at a grassy patch. Continue forward, keeping the River Clachaig in sight. At 566349, ford the Allt Beithe and keep ahead on a diminishing path. The path ahead, up the side of the glen is discernible from here.

G Pass through boggy grass to approach the river, until a small cairn on a grassy patch on the western river bank denotes a ford. In flood conditions, you may have to wade across.

H Ascend the fairly well-defined path diagonally up the side of the glen to the bealach.

I Leave the bealach with its cairn and locate the descending path on the E side of the glen, which descends E of S. The path is well defined, but very wet in places.

J Pass through the gate to gain the course of the old road by the bridge at Teanga Brideig. The A849 is nearby.

WALK 12

Dun da Ghaoithe Ridge

Start:	Car park at Birds of Prey & Conservation Centre, Torosay, A849 south of Craignure (724349)
Finish:	A849 N of Craignure (679397)
Alternative finish:	A849 S of Craignure; the starting point (724349)
Distance:	13km (8 miles) (7.5km [4.7 miles] to the summit)
Route features:	Track, undefined paths and steep ridge; rough undefined descent
OS map:	Explorer 375 Isle of Mull East (East Sheet)

Perhaps the most pleasant – and certainly the most spectacular – way of approaching the Isle of Mull is via the 40-minute ferry trip from Oban on the mainland to Craignure on the island. As you sail across the Firth of Lorn the splendour of the island's east coast will unfold before you, the view ahead being dominated by the peaks and ridges of Dun da Ghaoithe – the best ridge walk on Mull.

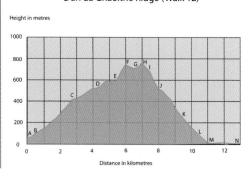

Dun da Ghaoithe Ridge (Walk 12)

CRAIGNURE

Shortly before the ferry arrives at Craignure you will pass Lismore to starboard, with its lighthouse on an adjacent island, and Duart Point to port. Perched atop the point is Duart Castle, an archetypal 13th-century Scottish fortress. The castle, open to the public, has had a chequered history, and is well worth investigating. It is the home of Sir Lachlen Maclean Bt, 28th Chief of the Clan Maclean.

On landing at Craignure you are within a few minutes' walk of the Old Pier Station. This is a terminus of the privately operated Mull and West Highland Narrow (260mm) Gauge Railway; a miniature steam- and diesel-hauled line. The trains will take you directly to Torosay Castle; not another fortification, but a 19th-century Scottish baronial mansion. It is the only castle to be served by its very own railway, and once inside the house visitors are invited to sit down on the many comfortable chairs and settees to rest, read a book or newspaper, or to enjoy the views over the splendid terraced gardens.

To find the start of the walk, travel south from Craignure on the A849 Fionnphort road, which soon brings you to the vehicular entrance to Torosay. About 200m further along the road you will see a sign inviting you to turn right to the Birds of Prey & Conservation Centre. Follow these directions, taking the right fork at the bottom a few metres from the A849. A short drive up a steep, well-made zigzag road will bring you to the centre's car park. You may park here, but a notice invites you to park tidily and to put a donation in the box provided if you are not visiting the centre.

From the car park, a right turn puts you onto the track leading to the centre and to our walk. Having climbed over a ladder stile next to a gate locked with a chain of 17 locks, the track to the summit, 700m higher, is relentlessly uphill. This is the access route to two sites, the first with two telecommunications towers and the second with one, all three sprouting many aerials. On the way up take time to enjoy the views over the Firth of Lorn towards Oban and Lorn itself, up Loch Linnhe towards the Ben Nevis massif and across the Sound of Mull to Morvern. You can see Duart Castle quite clearly, standing proud and menacing on the point. Torosay is hidden amongst trees. Calmac ferries glide silently across the waters, leaving phosphorescent wakes in the sea, which constantly changes colour. As you gain height, you will discover that Dun da Ghaoithe, at 766m the second highest hill in Mull, lives up to its name 'The Hill of Two Winds'. The formation of the peaks and ridges deflects the winds over the summit – at times it seems as though it should be upgraded to 'The Hill of Six Winds'! It can be very breezy up there, as witnessed by the many snow poles felled by the ferocity of the gales.

From the second telecommunications tower the route becomes almost totally undefined with only the occasional indication of a path. The way along the ridge is steep in parts, but not difficult. Given fair weather, the views over the water, across the mountain tops and into the glens are splendid. Eventually you will arrive at the OS trig point pillar. But do not be misled; neither this, nor the cairn a few metres away, is the main summit. The real summit is marked by another cairn, 1km northwest and a few metres higher.

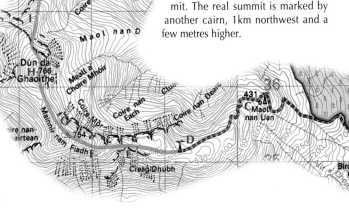

82

At the summit it is decision time. The quickest, and by far the easiest way down, is to retrace your steps. However, if you are an ambitious and strong walker with transport at the end, you can proceed ahead to descend on the broad east spur of Beinn Chreagach. The going is rough with, initially, no defined paths. Once you get to the gate in the fence, you can follow a track made by quad bikes down through the old wood and onto the forest road to join the A849 coast road. ▶

Route notes

A Leave the car park and turn right to join the access track to the telecommunications towers.

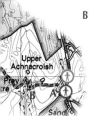

B Climb over the tall, steel ladder stile and continue on the track to the lower tower.

C Follow the track to the right to continue to the upper tower.

Dun da Ghaioithe Ridge and Duart Castle

There is a route from the summit of Dun da Ghaoithe along the ridge to Beinn Mheadhon, Beinn Chreagach and beyond, continuing the spectacular views over the Sound of Mull.

83

D The track ends here. Keep ahead and climb the small ridge to gradually ascend W. Occasional remnants of a path.

E Continue W on the broad ridge.

F Ascend steeply to the trig point and cairn. This is not the main summit. Continue NW, slightly descending on the broad ridge then:

G A steep climb over very stony ground.

H The final stretch – a few metres – to the summit is mainly grassy.

Either retrace your steps to the start, or:

I Leave the summit on the broad ridge NNW. Turn N to descend on the spur. No defined path after leaving the ridge. Take care amongst the rocky outcrops.

J Turn NE to descend on the broad E spur of Beinn Chreagach.

K Make for the gate in the fence at 686378. Then follow the path made by quad bikes.

L Cross the burn, keeping it on your left to continue the descent. Recross the burn to join the course of the old road, now a forest road.

N Join the A849.

WALK 13

Lochbuie to Carsaig

Start:	Lochbuie, on Loch Buie (608249); space between road and sea-shore
Finish:	Carsaig Pier (545213); very limited roadside parking
Distance:	9km (5.5 miles)
Route features:	Track and mainly undefined paths, very slow and rough going along sea-shore on shingle through rocks, bogs and occasional trees; rope-assisted short descent of rocky peninsula
OS map:	Explorer 375 Isle of Mull East (East & West Sheets)

As you approach Lochbuie you will be impressed by the comparative lushness of the vegetation. Indeed, until the 19th-century clearances, this 4000ha estate had some of the most fertile land on the island and was known as the Garden of Mull.

MULL'S STONE CIRCLE

You may wish to visit some of the local attractions while you're in the area. About 1km before reaching the coast you will cross a bridge on a bend spanning Abhainn a' Chaiginn Mhòir. There is parking space for two or three vehicles just before the bridge, and a sign indicating the way through a gate to the stone circle. The path, boggy in places, is marked by white stones and there are odd planks to help across the worst wet bits. There are eight stones standing in a circle, with a ninth marking the position of a lost stone. This is the only stone circle on Mull and, as usual, there is much conjecture about why Bronze Age man went to so much trouble.

To get to the starting point, take the A849 Fionnphort road southerly from Craignure. After about 10km, turn left onto a narrow unclassified road, signed Lochbuie. A further 12km, passing alongside Lochs Spelve and Uisg, will bring you to the hamlet of Lochbuie on the shores of Loch Buie itself. There are off-road parking spaces opposite the (closed) post office.

The walk to Carsaig is fairly short and quite delightful, but do not be misled by its brevity. Devoid of real navigational difficulties it may be, but the terrain in parts is such as to slow you down enormously (see below). Although OS Explorer maps show a path along the whole route, it is best done on an ebb tide in order to avoid too much scrambling amongst the rocks fallen from the crags above. You may wish to explore some of the caves along the route above you on the right, their height indicating where sea level used to be.

From the parking place, the walk starts off gently enough, along a reasonable track. After Glenbyre Farm only slow progress will be made due to the fact that you have to find your way amongst pebbles and boulders from the beach and rocks from the cliffs above. The high cliffs on your right reflect the sound of the sea crashing inland. Watch out for eagles and buzzards hovering in

MOY CASTLE

From the parking area at Lochbuie, you can drive or walk eastwards to view the ivy-clad, castellated remains of Moy Castle. Reputedly built by Hector Maclean in the early 15th century, it is more like a Borders bastle than a defensive castle. Abandoned in 1752 when a new mansion was built nearby, the castle is now kept securely locked as it is unsafe to enter. Its magnificent position, close to the loch with Ben Buie as a backdrop, does not betray the fact that inside is a dungeon designed to inflict the most terrible mental torment on prisoners. It is a bottle dungeon, the only access being through a hole in the floor of the castle. The wretched prisoner could only sit or stand, in total darkness, on a small projecting rock, surrounded by water 2.5m deep.

About 500m easterly from Moy Castle a track brings you to Laggan Sands, near the western end of which is a mausoleum built for the Maclaines of Lochbuie. This medieval building has been restored twice, most recently in 1972.

high places, and many seabirds. At **C** a fixed rope provides a hand hold on an easy descent down a 3m drop
over the edge of a small rocky peninsula, although in dry
conditions many walkers should be able to negotiate this
hazard without using the rope.

After the drop, the going is again slow amongst
shingle, rocks, bogs, grass, bracken and trees although,
in parts, planks and strategically placed stones help
the walker along. This continues until **F**, where there
is a good path all the way to the pier and road head at
Carsaig. If you linger awhile on the pier, you are likely
to be inspected by inquisitive seals basking in the still
waters of the loch.

Route notes

A Leave the parking area and walk westwards on the
lane, which degenerates into a track. Follow it
for about 3km to Glenbyre Farm.

B Pass behind (landward side) of
the farm, keeping the sheep
pens on your left. Pass
through two gates to

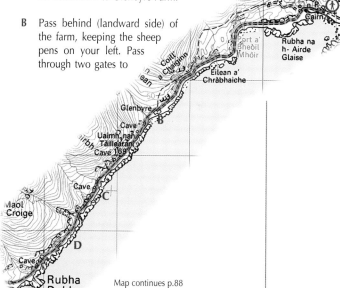

Map continues p.88

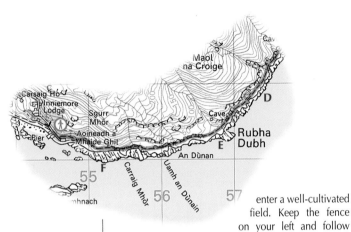

enter a well-cultivated field. Keep the fence on your left and follow it to a footbridge. Cross the bridge over Glenbyre Burn and pass through another gate. The path forward is fairly well defined, but in places is very rough going amongst seashore shingle and rocks.

C Use the rope to help descend the small rocky peninsula, noting the waterfall above right. Keep going on the ill-defined path, finding your way amongst boulders.

D A section of about 1km is very difficult going amongst rocks, boulders, bogs, grass, bracken and trees.

E The path becomes more defined as it passes through a broken fence with an iron kissing gate. Keep ahead. Very rough going.

F The going becomes easier on a well-defined path all the way to the pier and road head at Carsaig.

Denis Brook on rope down rocky peninsula

Walks in south Mull based on Bunessan

WALK 14

Carsaig Arches

Start & finish:	Carsaig Pier (545213); very limited roadside parking
Distance:	13.5km (8 miles) return
Route features:	Track and mainly undefined, very slow and rough going along sea-shore on shingle through rocks and bogs
OS map:	Explorers 375 Isle of Mull East (West Sheet) & 373 Iona, Staffa & Ross of Mull

This is one of the classic walks on Mull and is relatively short. However, do not be misled by its apparent brevity, as the going is very rough in places. The scenery is breathtaking, with pounding waves to the left and 220m-high cliffs to the right. You will be treated to many wonderful sights, including fertile farmland and spectacular cliff formations with many caves, high up due to the lowering of sea levels. Basalt columns are everywhere. Herons, gulls, buzzards and eagles abound, and you may even notice wild goats observing your progress from their craggy vantage points.

To get to the starting point take the A849 Craignure road easterly from Bunessan. After about 15km, turn right at Pennyghael onto a narrow, unclassified road, signed Carsaig. A further 7km will bring you to Carsaig Pier, where there is space for parking several cars. The last 0.75km or so of this drive is especially narrow, winding and steep, as the road dips over the edge of the cliffs into the vast amphitheatre of Carsaig Bay. If you get to the pier early in the day you should have no parking problems, but this is a popular place and the spaces tend to be filled by lunchtime.

THE NUN'S CAVE

It is said that during the Reformation nuns fled Iona Abbey, came over the pass and hid in the Nuns' Cave. To this day, early Christian religious carvings are to be seen on the walls of the cave; some are said to date back to the 6th century. This tradition of leaving one's mark lives on with contemporary graffiti. The shallow cave is in a sandstone measure, topped by basalt columns. In the late 1400s and early 1500s monks from Iona quarried the sea-washed stone from the shore and used the shallow cave as a shelter for working the stone into embellishments and gravestones for the abbey. The bankers (masons' workbenches) are still evident near the cave. The masons not only left their marks on the worked stone, but also on the cave walls. The quarry was used intermittently until the late 1800s, when it was finally closed after stone was quarried and dressed for use in the restoration of the abbey.

OS Explorer maps show a path all the way from Carsaig Pier to the arches, but the walk is best done on an ebb tide to avoid too much scrambling amongst rocks beneath the towering cliffs.

Carsaig Arches

From the pier, the walking is initially easy, following a track through trees to the shore. Fighting your way through prickly gorse bushes at **B** can be avoided by walking through the field on your right. At **D**, the

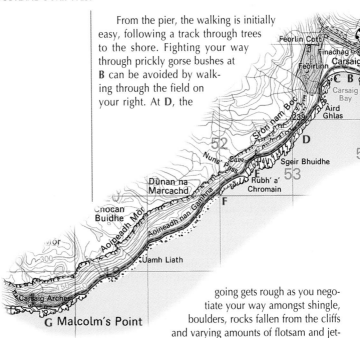

going gets rough as you negotiate your way amongst shingle, boulders, rocks fallen from the cliffs and varying amounts of flotsam and jetsam. Occasional strategically placed planks and stones help the way through some of the more boggy patches.

As you near **E**, Rubh' a' Chromain (Point of the Hawk), you will see ahead a huge weather-sculptured rock marking the Nuns' Pass.

The walk continues to be very rough going and the path ill defined. Malcolm's Point at 495184 (Malcolm was one of St Columba's followers), signifies that you have arrived at the arches, and the path ends abruptly at a cave. Here, the cliffs of columnar basalt soar to a height of 240m. The sea below crashes along the rocky shore towards the first massive arch, 20m high, 20m wide and 43m long. These spectacular rock formations are a result of sea caves being eroded by the power-house forces of countless tides. It is possible to see the second arch, by retracing one's steps a few paces and taking the path which rises high above and over the first arch and on down to the shore. This path is narrow and exposed and not for the inexperienced or faint-hearted walker. It is the only way to get down to the beach and inspect both arches from close quarters, but should not be used in inclement weather.

Route notes

A Leave the parking area and walk down the track which slips away from the road above the pier buildings and descends to the shore.

B A gate on the left gives access to the shore. After a few hundred metres, gorse bushes impede the way. Use the stiles on the right to access the field to bypass this hazard.

C Use one of the stiles to get back to the shore path, and continue through the metal kissing gate.

D From here the path becomes very rough, alternating between grassy paths and seashore boulders, Very slow going. Very, very rough.

E Visit the Nuns' Cave if you wish. Then continue ahead on the path, which varies in definition.

F Navigation is straightforward, but the way is very rough and ill defined in places.

G Carsaig Arches form a barrier to further progress, except to very experienced walkers.

Return by the same route.

WALK 15

MacCulloch's Fossil Tree

Start & finish:	Primitive car park on the Tiroran estate (478275)
Distance:	20km (12.4 miles) return
Route features:	Track, path and narrow goat/sheep trod along very steep hillside leading to difficult approach to 6m ladder descent; sea-shore walk to tree among very rough shingle, boulders and through seaweed
OS map:	Explorer 375 Isle of Mull East (West Sheet)

The walk to the fossil tree is perhaps the most challenging in this book. It is also possibly the most exhilarating. Not for the faint-hearted, it should only be attempted by fit and experienced walkers. Time your walk carefully, ideally starting on an ebb tide to ensure your arrival at the tree coincides with, or is near to, low water. The round trip is a whole day's walk, sometimes over difficult terrain, so plan well and enjoy the experience.

MULL'S VOLCANIC PAST

About 50 million years ago, in the Eocene epoch, the area now known as Mull was a huge forest and home to an abundance of creatures. Early forms of horses and bats were plentiful, and whales ruled the seas. Lava flows were frequent, with numerous volcanoes spewing out their contents far and wide. On the Ardmeanach peninsula many trees became engulfed in the molten fire flows, yet some were massive enough to actually cool the lava that surrounded them. Relatively recently, in 1819, the fossil remains of one such tree were discovered by a Dr MacCulloch, whose name has been given to this wonder of the geological world.

To find the starting point, drive easterly along the A849 Craignure road from Bunessan. After about 20km, make

a left turn on to the B8035. A further 6.5km brings you to a left turn on to an unclassified road, signed Tiroran. The car park is another 2.5km on, shortly after passing through the gates of the Tiroran estate.

Basalt columns on seashore

In Gaelic, the Ardmeanach peninsula is called Innis Iar, which means 'Western Pasture'. This idyllic-sounding description does not accurately reflect the true nature of this fierce and remote place: its common name 'The Wilderness' is far more appropriate.

The walk starts sedately enough on a good wide track, passing to the left of Tavool House at **C**. After a further 0.5km a gate gives access to land owned by the National Trust for Scotland. This quiet, isolated part of the peninsula was donated to the Trust in 1932. The path is still well defined, but can be very muddy in places. Burg Farmhouse at **D** is your last connection with habitation until your return, and some people knock on the door to advise the owners of their intention to visit the tree. You may care to do the same.

On the horizon ahead you will see the distinctive shape of Dun Bhuirg. Duns, small defensive forts, were built towards the end of the Ice Age, often as showpiece

DAISY CHEAPE

Whilst Dun Bhuirg itself has been reduced to piles of stones outlining no more than its original circular form, it is worth paying a short visit to read the memorial to Daisy Cheape, clearly visible inside the remains of the dun. Twelve-year-old Daisy, whose family owned the Carsaig and Tiroran estates, set out on a boat trip to Carsaig with her brothers on 15 August 1896. A storm overtook them and the boat capsized. The boys and the boatmen survived, but Daisy drowned.

homes, by leaders of tribes. In its prominent position, the dun overlooks Port na Croise (Port of the Crossing) on the coast below Burg. The port was probably an embarkation point for the crossing of Loch Scridain to Ardchrichnich on the north coast of the Ross of Mull.

At **F**, the path descends to the shingle beach. Do not relax yet – the walk is about to become a little more difficult.

At **G**, the narrow path, perhaps a goat track on the very steep hillside, passes amongst fallen rocks. You may see eagles and buzzards soaring to dizzy heights on the uplifting thermals. Wild goats may pose on craggy viewpoints. Looking down, you will see many structures of columnar basalt laid out on the rocky shores in fantastical formations.

At **H** great care is needed as the steep and narrow path descends the hillside to end abruptly at the top of a 6m-long steel ladder. The ladder, leaning against the rock face, is robust and firmly fixed. There is no hand hold at the top and little room for manoeuvre. Take extra care when you descend. From the foot of the ladder there is yet another scramble down the steep rocks to the seashore below.

About 0.5km away you will see the first of twin waterfalls streaming over the edge of the cliffs, and these mark the site of the fossil tree. The going along the beach is difficult amongst shingle, pebbles, rocks and seaweed.

MACCULLOCH'S TREE

MacCulloch's Tree (about 12m high and 1.5m in diameter) and its surroundings are spectacular. When the tree was engulfed with molten lava, all those millions of years ago, its bulk was sufficient to cool the lava immediately surrounding it. The basalt twisted into amazing, almost unbelievable shapes. Over the years the tree became a fossil, most of which disappeared with the passage of time, eroded from the top by natural causes. Since its whereabouts became public knowledge in the beginning of the 19th century the attentions of 'souvenir hunters' have reduced the fossil yet further, leaving a 1m-high section at the base, including a portion of charcoal. The contour of the original 12m-high fossil remains clearly visible in the rock face.

MacCulloch's Fossil Tree

Your arrival at the tree, just around the corner from the second waterfall, deserves to be heralded with a fanfare of trumpets and celebrated with a free glass of champagne. More likely is the echoing of the sea breaking on the rocks, the raucous cries of seabirds and a taste of salty air.

When you have had your fill of admiring and recording this remote rarity, your return journey is less demanding as the ascent of the ladder is easier than the descent. We do not advise exploring the headland beyond the tree. Only the shore is navigable with great difficulty and only at low water.

If you called at Burg on your way out to tell them of your visit, let them know of your return.

Route notes

A   Leave the car park, taking the track westerly.

B   Keep right at the bifurcation to ascend. Continue on the well-defined track to Tavool House.

C   Below the house, where the main track ascends, keep left on the grassy track, with the grounds of the house on your right, and follow this to the farmhouse at Burg. Wet potholes make the progress slower.

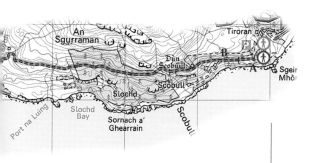

D   Pass below the farmhouse, continuing on the less well-defined track towards the prominent dun. Pass the dun on the path starting to descend. The path is well defined but is wet in places and involves the crossing of burns.

E   The path is now almost at sea level, still well defined just above the seashore.

F   The path becomes more difficult, ascending and descending on the steep hillside to follow the lie of the land and passing amongst fallen rocks.

G   The path becomes an exposed scramble down to the top of the ladder. The ladder is very robust and safe, but requires great care in descent. The descent from the foot of the ladder to the shore is a steep scramble. The fossil tree is about 0.5km along the shore. The only route is to navigate your way through shingle, pebbles, rocks and seaweed. Very difficult going.

H   Identify two waterfalls tumbling from the cliff top, then proceed around the rocks to get to the tree. Very difficult going.

Return by the same route.

IONA

Sandy west coast of Iona (Walk 16A)

As Iona is very small, being some 5km by 2.5km, we have recorded two short walks, which should give you a good appreciation of this fascinating place.

Fionnphort, pronounced 'Feenfort', the ferry terminal to Iona, is about 60km by road from Craignure. Coaches meet the Oban ferries at the Craignure terminal to take visitors to Fionnphort, and it may be possible to get a seat on one of these. If you are interested, try asking at the TIC, but you may find that the last return coach is too early for your liking. If you use your own transport, be aware that no visitors' vehicles are allowed on Iona; the ferry across to Baile Mòr (Big Town) takes pedestrians only.

GRASS POINT

About 5km down the A849 from Craignure you will pass a sign indicating a minor road to Grass Point on the east coast. This, the nearest point on Mull to Oban, was once the ferry terminal, and in the 18th and early part of the 19th centuries was the point of embarkation for cattle which drovers had escorted across the island. The cattle were shipped over to the island of Kerrera, and then swam across to the mainland. In earlier times it was also the start of the Pilgrims' Way, marked by a line of stones all the way to Fionnphort. About 3.5km down the coast from Grass Point is Port nam Marbh (Port of the Dead) where, years ago, cortèges carrying the bodies of dignitaries from the mainland started their journeys across Mull to Iona.

FIONNPHORT

Whilst in Fionnphort there are two short excursions which may offer a pleasant diversion. A turn northwards for a couple of kilometres on the A849 from the ferry terminal will, after 3km or so, bring you to the delightful hamlet of Kintra, another one-time landing place for cattle from the outer islands. With a few houses and parking space for only two or three cars, it provides a base for exploring the bays and inlets of this secluded part of the north coast of the Ross of Mull. The views out to Staffa are quite spectacular. There are, however, no pubs, shops or facilities of any sort in Kintra – nothing but tranquil scenery.

An additional exploration is to take the road southwards from Fionnphort. The road head at Knockvologan will be reached after a drive of about 9km from the visitor centre. After passing through the gate, a short walk along the track will bring you to Erraid Sound, the sands of which can be safely crossed (for two hours only) at low water. Erraid is an island with strong literary associations. It is said to resemble the Treasure Island made famous by Robert Louis Stevenson. Some say that it is also the island where David Balfour, hero of *Kidnapped*, spent a few forlorn days. Remember to make sure of your return crossing by referring to the tide tables, so as not to re-enact David Balfour's experiences.

From Bunessan, the ferry car park is 10km westerly on the A849. The ferry across the Sound of Iona runs at frequent intervals, taking about 15 minutes depending

Stone-saw frame at Iona marble quarry (Walk 16B)

on weather conditions. Should you wish to base yourself here for a few days in order to visit the abbey and generally explore, there are B&Bs on both sides of the Sound and a couple of hotels on Iona.

WALK 16A

Baile Mòr (1)

Start & finish:	Jetty at Baile Mòr (286240); cars to be left in ferry car park on mainland of Mull
Distance:	4km (2.5 miles) return
Route features:	Road and well-defined rough path
OS map:	Explorer 373 Iona, Staffa & Ross of Mull

The first walk takes you to the highest point on the island, the top of Dun I, pronounced 'Dun Ee' (101m).

From the vantage point of Dun I – the spot visited by Columba – you can get an overview of the whole area: pure white sandy beaches to the north, the Sound of Iona to the east, heather-fringed hills to the south and springy machair on yet more beaches to the west. Given suitable weather conditions, you should be able to see the 175km-long stretch of the Inner Hebrides from Skye to Islay. A small-scale map will be useful in identifying the many islands. The walking is easy and uncomplicated.

Route notes

A Leave the jetty and ascend the road ahead.

B Turn right with the road.

C   Follow the road past the abbey.

Sound of Iona with boats

D   Just beyond the entrance to the row of three houses with seven gabled dormer windows, leave the road through the kissing gate on the left and ascend the pathless field. Aim for the foot of the rocky outcrop of Dun I.

E   Follow the rough path to the summit.

Return by the same route. If you wish to visit the northern beach at Tràigh Bhàn, turn left on your return to the road. The beach is about 1km to the north.

WALK 16B

Baile Mòr (2)

Start & finish:	Jetty at Baile Mòr (286240); cars to be left in ferry car park on mainland of Mull
Distance:	8.5km (5.3 miles)
Route features:	Road and mainly undefined rough paths; sometimes very wet and boggy on rough return route
OS map:	Explorer 373 Iona, Staffa & Ross of Mull

Having completed the first walk, you may wish to explore further. This route takes you to the west coast, down to the south coast and back to the starting point.

From the ferry, a short walk on well-surfaced roads brings you towards the western part of the island. After passing through a gate, you will find yourself walking across the springy machair of common grazing land (**C**). This is actually the island's sheep-grazed nine-hole golf course. Not much use for lawn mowers here. After turning south at **D**, a spouting cave can be seen in the distance near an overhanging cliff. Given a good westerly wind (not difficult on this coast) with plenty of white horses at sea, the spout can be quite spectacular, with its plume of spray rising high up the cliffs.

After passing Loch Staoineig (**G**), the path descends to the pebbly beach (**H**) at Port na Curaich.

Leaving the bay, the path becomes non-existent through grass and heather. Keep near to the coastline, minding the rocky inlets. The ruins at **K** were once the walls of quarry workers' shelters. A short scramble down into the gully will reveal the remains of a gas engine and a stone-saw frame. A tiny jetty is still apparent with

ST COLUMBA'S BAY

The Gaelic for Port na Curaich translates to Port of the Coracle, but it is more popularly known as St Columba's Bay, for it was here that Columba landed in AD563. It is said that he first landed at the Garvellach Isles in the Firth of Lorn, but as he was still able to see the hills of Ireland from this landing place he decided to move on to Iona. There is a long, low pile of pebbles on the beach, supposed to represent the size of Columba's coracle. Some coracles (or currochs) in those days were quite substantial sea-going vessels complete with sails. The origins of the other piles of shingle are uncertain, but it has been suggested that monks built these as cairns in penance for their sins, the size of the mounds being proportionate to the severity of their transgressions.

rusty ironware to which boats bringing in men and materials and taking out marble could be tied. Last worked between 1907 and 1915, the quarries produced some superb marble. A prime example is the abbey altar, veined with beautiful green serpentine.

From the quarries a path to the north is clearly visible, but soon disappears into the boggy peat. Using Dun I as a marker, find the fence and follow it to return to Baile Mòr and the ferry.

Pebble cross at St Columba's Bay

Route notes

A On leaving the ferry, turn left to follow the metalled road, passing a restaurant on your left and shop on your right.

B Turn right with the road and follow it for rather more than 1km.

C The metalling ceases. Pass through the gate onto common grazing land, keeping ahead towards the sea.

D After about 200m, turn left and follow the barely discernible track in the grass, heading generally S.

E Pass in front of the house (Culdamh) about 100m away to your left.

F Descend into the gully with a small watercourse on

the very rough path. A cubic concrete hut appears. Pass this, and ascend the very rough track.

G   Keep Loch Staoineig on your right, following the path.

H   Continue on the defined path, duly descending to the sea at:

I   Leave the sea eastwards to scramble up the rocky outcrop.

J   Turn NE, no defined path amongst the grass and heather.

K   Turn E and descend to pass the ruins of buildings.

L   Turn S to descend the gully to the sea to view the remains of the marble quarries at 268217. Return up the gully and proceed more or less due N.

M   No formal path. Many sheep trods. Turn E of N.

N   An old fence appears. Follow this through very boggy ground, keeping the fence on your left.

O   Leave the fence and go roughly NE to locate the gate, which exits the common grazing land.

P   Pass through the gate to follow the track to the road at:

Q   Cross the road and continue on a gravelled track.

R   Pass through the gate into the farmyard of Maol. Turn right behind the farmhouse and follow the descending track.

S   Turn right to join the metalled road and descend to the jetty.

MORVERN, ARDGOUR, SUNART AND ARDNAMURCHAN

Loch Shiel from Resipole (Hill Walk 10)

Loch Sunart from Resipol (Walk 12)

Morvern, Ardgour, Sunart and Ardnamurchan can hardly claim to trip off the tongues of strangers. Yet stay for a while and they will win your heart and give you images to dream of when back in the saddle of your daily round. Surrounding Loch Sunart, these delightful areas provide a wide variety of walking to suit every taste, from the stimulating to the very restful.

Whilst exploring the island of Mull, you cannot fail to notice that across the shimmering waters of the Sound of Mull lies the mainland. The small MacBrayne car and passenger ferry from Fishnish Pier on the island will take you to the village of Lochaline in the district of Morvern on the mainland.

Leaving the ferry terminal and turning right on the A884 you will cross the open moorland of Morvern, and after about 30km will arrive at the head of Loch Sunart.

LOCHALINE'S QUARRIES

Within sight of the ferry terminal at Lochaline are the workings of sand quarries. During World War II these were Britain's only source of the fine grade silica sand used to make optical glass, and today over 40km of tunnels are still worked. Whilst the quarry entrances, the screens, washers and conveyors do nothing to enhance the countryside, they do provide work in an area with little else, other than forestry, to employ the local labour force.

A right turn here leads to the Corran ferry, and a left will take you alongside Loch Sunart.

Ardgour – possibly meaning 'Promontory of the Goat' – is diamond shaped and almost isolated by its surrounding waters: Loch Eil in the north, Loch Linnhe to the east, Loch Shiel to the west and Glen Tarbert and Loch Sunart to the south. Public roads run around most of the perimeter, except by Loch Shiel. Until 1967 MacBrayne's ferries plied the waters of the loch, providing a valuable service to local inhabitants and visitors. The service was discontinued when a new forestry road made it redundant. We did discover, though, that a cruise service has recently opened, operating from Glenfinnan.

Although the topography of the area excludes any roads in the hinterland, it is possible to explore the delightful glens and mountain tops on foot. There is a sprinkling of Corbetts and several Donalds, but if you are looking for Munros you will not find them here. Any passion for great heights must be assuaged, for the time being, by the magnificent panorama of the Ben Nevis massif and the Appin Hills across Loch Linnhe.

Lochaline ferry

WALKS IN MORVERN, ARDGOUR, SUNART AND ARDNAMURCHAN
(Walks 1–18)

Corran ferry

Perhaps the quickest way of approaching Ardgour is by way of the Corran ferry, south of Fort William, taking just five minutes to cross the narrows of Loch Linnhe. At Corran you can turn right to visit north Ardgour, going north and west towards Glenfinnan, or you can turn left to go south and west to south Ardgour and on to Salen.

The southern road passes through Inversanda and down Glen Tarbert, where on the south side of the A851 lies the open moorland of **Morvern**. To the north is Garbh Bheinn (885m), a fine mountain to climb if you want a magnificent overview of Ardgour (and Morvern). About 20km from Loch Linnhe you will meet the head of Loch Sunart and the village of Strontian (Sron an-t Sidean or 'The Point of the Fairies').

Between Strontian and Salen – a distance of 16km – the road winds along the beautiful shores of Loch Sunart. Beinn Resipol (at 846m almost a Munro), in the district of **Sunart**, lies to the north. The climb to the top of this mountain is well rewarded as one is treated to stunning views over the relatively low-lying Ardnamurchan Peninsula and beyond. Loch Moidart points northwest to the isles of Muck, Eigg and Rhum. North-northeast the blue-black pinnacles of the Black Cuillin of Skye reach for the heavens. Beyond them – if the weather and

STRONTIAN

Strontian is a surprising place in that it has several quite elegant residences, rather than the serried rows of small cottages one might expect of a small Scottish village. The reason lies in the village's history of lead mining and the metallic element Strontium (Sr), atomic number 38. In 1793 Dr Thomas Charles Hope, a Scottish chemist, recognised a new rare earth here and named it Strontianite. In 1808 Humphry Davy isolated the element Strontium, the oxide of which burns with a brilliant crimson flame and is used in the manufacture of, amongst other things, fireworks. The famous Strontium 90, an isotope of Strontium, occurs as a by-product of nuclear fission. The lead mines were closed in 1904, reopened later, then closed again. Their remains serve to remind visitors of the once-thriving industry that brought prosperity to the village. Strontian's other claim to fame is that it once had a floating church. In the mid 1800s, the estate owners refused to give the Free Church a plot of land on which to build a place of worship. In desperation, the local folk had a boat converted into a church by the Clyde shipbuilders and towed it round to an anchorage at Ardnastang on Loch Sunart. The church was well patronised. The estate later relented and a 'land church' was built nearby. The remains of the jetty for the floating church can still be seen on the shores of the loch, but unfortunately the church, just below the Ben View Hotel, is in a sad state of repair and at the time of writing has been offered for sale.

Loch Sunart shore

Loch Sunart from Ardnastang

visibility are exceptionally good – you can see the islands of the Outer Hebrides. This is a place where a small-scale map can really be of benefit as an aid to identifying the long-range views. Not only known for its magnificent vistas, Resipol has a rich history of ancient coffin routes as well as the more recent lead-mining activities. There are many walks on and around this mountain and we have chosen three for you to explore.

At Salen, the road goes northwards to Acharacle and on into **Moidart**. All the land to the west is **Ardnamurchan**, reaching 27km towards the Atlantic. Turning left at Salen, the road to the point becomes even narrower than hitherto, winding around the contours of the rugged coastline, occasionally turning inland to avoid mountains such as Ben Hiant – the Holy Mountain (528m) – with its jagged ramparts of volcanic rock. The road is fringed with scrub oak trees and crags, and moss-covered stone walls outlining the banks of the loch. Alongside the road from Sunart to Ardnamurchan are many delightful woodland and coastal walks. Each is only 2 or 3km long, well signed, and with information boards giving historical information about the area. Full details can be obtained at the Strontian TIC.

Devoid of the visitor attractions of Lands End, lonely and quite unspoiled – and 37km further west – the Point of Ardnamurchan is the true most westerly point of the British mainland. The point has a lighthouse, approached by a traffic-light controlled single-lane carriageway. It has a small tearoom and a museum, which depicts life in the lighthouse when it was a manned operation. The lighthouse – built between 1844 and 1854 from Mull granite by Alan Stevenson (uncle of Robert Louis) – bears more than a passing resemblance to the monument where Prince Charlie raised his standard at Glenfinnan in 1745. The 36m-high granite tower, the only one in Britain to be built in an Egyptian style, stands on an 18m-high cliff, the fully automated brightly burning light being visible for nearly 30km.

Northeast of the point are several beaches, many with the pure white shell sands for which Ardnamurchan has become justifiably famous. Some are accessible by road, most on foot; some have been spoiled by holiday homes, some remain pristine.

Be sure to visit Kentra Bay and Sanna Bay. Sanna is really four separate sandy bays with low cliffs housing

Descent to Loch Laga (Walk 14)

ARDNAMURCHAN

Ardnamurchan (possibly meaning 'Promontory of the Otters') is not without its historical reminders. About 1km before Kilchoan – the principal village of western Ardnamurchan – lies the ruin of Mingary Castle. On the water's edge, it guards the entrances to the Sound of Mull and Loch Sunart. Probably built by the Maclains of Ardnamurchan in the 13th century, the castle has suffered the attacks of various clans, not to mention an unsuccessful siege by troops from an Armada galleon in Tobermory Bay. After many additions and much restoration, the castle – which features in Scott's narrative poem *The Lord of the Isles* – was last inhabited late in the 19th century. There is a fine view of the ruins from the Kilchoan to Tobermory ferry terminal. Other historical sites include Greadal Fhinn (Fingal's Griddle), the site of a prehistoric stone circle. Do not be misled, however, by Glenborrodale Castle. This is a modern hotel, built early in the 20th century on the site of a much earlier stronghold.

Foghorn and lighthouse at Point of Ardnamurchan (Walk 17)

the Glendrian Caves, which can only be seen at low tide. The sea in this area appears to be a luminous green because of the pure white sandy seabed. Also deserving a visit, Kilmory and Achatory beaches are renowned for their excellent and rare seashells.

The once-thriving fishing industry in Ardnamurchan was destroyed by the Clearances, by the lack of herring and by poaching. Scattered around this remote area, a few farms, several crofts, some salmon farming and forestry operations as well as the tourist trade now provide work for the small communities.

WALK 1

Ardtornish Point

Start & finish:	Acranich, E of Kinlochaline Castle, off A884 N of Lochaline (702474); roadside parking
Distance:	13km (8.1 miles) return
Route features:	Private, sometimes surfaced road, followed by well-defined path to castle and point
OS map:	Explorer 383 Morvern & Lochaline (West Sheet)

This walk beside the loch is straightforward and not difficult. As the village of Lochaline comes into view across the loch you will probably see ships being loaded with silica sand from the quarries. You may also see the ferry boats plying between Lochaline and Fishnish on the Isle of Mull making regular calls at the jetty. From here, your route turns southeast to follow the shore of the Sound of Mull.

To find the starting point, turn right off the A884 about 4km north of Lochaline. After passing Kinlochaline Castle on your left, you will shortly arrive at the entrance to the private road, on the right, which follows the east shore of Loch Aline. There is room to park your vehicle near the entrance.

The 15th-century Kinlochaline Castle, standing prominently on a crag at the head of Loch Aline was, at one time, the seat of the Clan MacInnes. The castle was restored in 1890 but is not open to the public.

OS Explorer maps show a path from the farm buildings near Ardtornish Castle – at the furthest point of the walk – continuing along the coast, but it does not appear on the ground.

ARDTORNISH CASTLE

Ardtornish Castle, unlike Kinlochaline Castle, is now a complete ruin. Allegedly built by John, the first Lord of the Isles, in the 14th century, it became the seat of future Lords. It was here that John II, the last of the Lords, signed the Treaty of Ardtornish. The co-signatory was Edward IV of England and it was supposed to arrange 'the dismembership of Scotland'. When discovered, the conspiracy led to the downfall of John. The castle was owned by MacLean of Duart in the 17th century, after which it remained unoccupied. As there is no record of its being destroyed in battle, presumably it fell into ruin. There is now little to be seen of the original architecture, but the massive basement walls of the quadrilateral keep survive as a reminder of its heritage. There are fine views across the Sound of Mull.

Ardtornish Castle

The return journey to Kinlochaline allows you to see the loch and its surroundings from a different perspective, and the approach to Kinlochaline Castle and Ardtornish House with its Scottish turrets is particularly photogenic.

Route notes

A   Leave the public road at 702474. Follow the private road alongside Loch Aline.

B   Keep going.

C   At the farm buildings, keep right to the gate, partially hidden by trees, which gives access to a path.

D   Follow the defined path to Ardtornish Point and the castle.

Return by the same route.

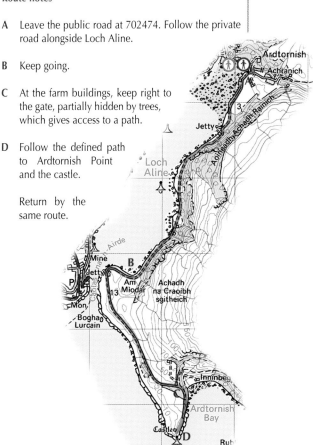

WALK 2

Achranich to Loch Teàrnait

Start & finish: Acranich, E of Kinlochaline Castle, off A884 north of
Lochaline (702474); roadside parking
Distance: 10km (6.2 miles) return
Route features: Well-defined track all the way
OS map: Explorer 383 Morvern & Lochaline (West Sheet)

This is a short, easy walk along a well-defined track which, as it presents no
difficulties, can easily be done in a morning or afternoon.

To find the starting point, turn right off the A884 about
4km north of Lochaline. After passing Kinlochaline
Castle on your left, you will shortly arrive at the entrance
to the private road, on the right, which follows the east
shore of Loch Aline. There is room to park your vehicle
near the entrance.

Loch Teàrnait is quite large, about 1km long by
0.5km wide. It is delightfully situated, high in the surrounding hills, and even has its own tiny historical island.
On a warm, sunny day, what could be more delightful
than sitting beside the loch enjoying the air, the hills
and perhaps a picnic. On both sides of the loch there is

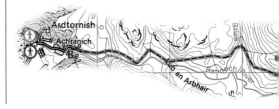

BOTHY CODE

Respect other users

- Leave the bothy clean, tidy and with dry kindling wood for the next visitors

Respect the bothy

- Guard against fire risk and don't cause vandalism or graffiti
- Take away all rubbish that you don't burn
- Avoid burying rubbish – this pollutes the environment
- Don't leave perishable food – this encourages mice and rats

Respect the surroundings

- Human waste must be buried carefully out of sight – please use the spade provided
- For health reasons, never use the vicinity of the bothy as a toilet and keep well away from the water supply
- Conserve fuel
- Never cut live wood.
- Finally, please ensure the fire is out and the door properly closed when you leave.

evidence of paths, shown on OS Explorer, going over to Loch Linnhe.

The bothy at Leacraithnaich overlooking the loch is, of course, open to all. Like all bothies maintained by the Mountain Bothies Association (MBA) it is only available for short stays, normally of a few days. Unless the safety of a group requires the use of shelter in bad weather,

bothies are not available for large groups of six or more because of overcrowding and lack of facilities such as toilets. For the same reasons, groups are asked not to camp outside bothies.

If you do use this – or any – bothy, please abide by the Bothy Code.

Route notes

A   Leave the parking area and continue on the metalled road to and through the estate yard. Beyond the yard, turn left and cross the bridge over the Rannoch River.

B   Turn right and follow the ascending track near the river. The water pipeline feeding the mini hydro-electric power station ends at the dam after about 1km. Follow the track all the way to Loch Teàrnait.

C   Keep left at the fork to get to Leacraithnaich, a bothy overlooking the loch.

Return by the same route.

WALK 3

Drimnin to Loch Teacuis

Start:	Bonnavoulin, NW of Lochaline (561537); roadside parking
Finish:	Road head near Kinlochteacuis, between Lochs Teacuis and Doire nam Mart (656542); roadside parking
Distance:	12km (7.5 miles)
Route features:	Road, track and path (sometimes ill defined)
OS map:	Explorer 383 Morvern & Lochaline (West Sheet)

Much of this walk is in forests. Forestry, crofting and the silica sand quarries of Lochaline plus a little tourism provide much-needed work for the sparse population of Morvern.

To get to the starting point, follow the B849 from Lochaline, with the Sound of Mull on your left, for about 19km. Along the way you will catch glimpses of Mull, a mere 3 or 4km across the Sound. You will also pass some

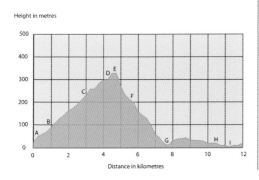

Drimnin to Loch Teacuis (Walk 3)

Rock formation on road to Drimnin

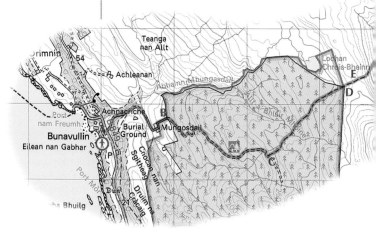

interesting rock formations and a castle. Park (tidily) on the roadside near the minor crossroads at Bonnavoulin almost, but not quite, at the end of the road.

The walk starts by passing through Mungosdail Farm (**B**) which, at the end of the 18th century, was the site of some corn mills and a kiln. A few years later its inhabitants fell victim to the Clearances. They were evicted to make way for the 'big sheep', the Cheviots, a move designed by the landowners to make themselves ever more prosperous.

After emerging from the forest at the end of the walk (**I**), you will pass a residence – once a school – at Ardantiobairt (just before arriving at the public road near Kinlochteacuis). From here you can drive to the A884 (about 7km southeast), to Lochaline or Strontian.

Map continues p.128

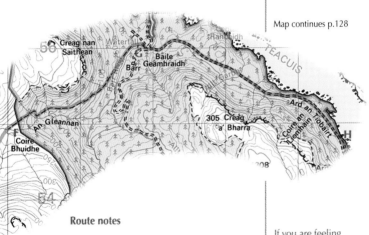

Route notes

A Leave the B849 up the track to Mungosdail Farm. Ascend through the farmyard.

B Enter the forest through the gate in the deer fence. The way is well defined all the way through the forest. Keep ascending.

If you are feeling particularly fit, and have time, you can continue from Kinlochteacuis and walk to Laudale (see Walk 4).

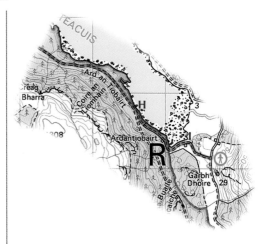

C At 583533 turn left to leave the forest road and ascend the path up the ride.

D Leave the forest through the gate and continue to ascend. The path becomes ill defined or non-existent.

E Pass over the bealach, then descend NNE. No defined path.

F Enter the forest at 601550. Follow the well-defined path descending through the forest.

G At the forest road, turn right and, after 100m or so, cross the bridge to continue on the forest road.

H At 645549, fork left to descend on the original forest road to the loch side.

I Emerge from the forest through the gate and continue on the track all the way to the public road at 656542.

WALK 4

Loch Teacuis to Laudale

Start:	Road near Kinlochteacuis, between Lochs Teacuis and Doire nam Mart (656542); roadside parking
Finish:	Road head near Laudale House on Loch Sunart (756599); roadside parking
Distance:	19.5km (12.1 miles) via shoreline; 18.5km (11.5 miles) via Glen Cripesdale
Route features:	Rough, boggy and pathless ascent; steep descent to defined forest tracks; some waymarkers. Last part of route on shore track; optional route on well-defined tracks/paths sometimes wet
OS map:	Explorer 383 Morvern & Lochaline (West Sheet)

Before reaching the road head near Kinlochteacuis you will find the remains of the village of Inniemore on the left, uncovered by forestry operations. This victim of the Clearances is clearly signposted and there is a car park and information board.

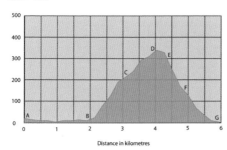

Loch Teacuis to Laudale (Walk 4)

(Loch Teacuis to Glencripesdale House)

Height in meteres

*Waymarker near
Bealach Sloc an Eich
with Loch Teacuis*

To get to the road head near Loch Teacuis, drive about 5km north from Lochaline and take the left turn into a minor road off the A884 just before Claggan. This narrow road passes to the southwest of Loch Arienas, where you may see a flock of huge, curly-horned rams. Near Kinlochteacuis there are various places to park off-road.

The early part of the route from Loch Teacuis (**B** & **C**) follows a simple but boggy and steep route, defined by waymarks. Be wary on the descent to Loch Sunart (**E**) – it is very steep and rocky. Once in the forest, follow the waymarks, being aware of possible forestry operations. On arriving at Glencripesdale House (**G**) you have the choice of two routes.

Loch Teacuis to Laudale (Walk 4)

(Glencripesdale House to Loch Sunart)

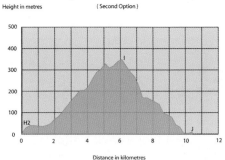

Height in metres   (Second Option)

Distance in kilometres

STONE SEATS

From this point you will encounter several stone built seats, spaced out over 3km or so, the last one overlooking Lochan Dhonnachaidh. It is thought that the seats, made to accommodate two or three persons, were built by a one-time owner of the big house to afford resting places for the ladies on their way to watch the men fishing in Lochan Dhonnachaidh. Nowadays they can be quite handy for any weary walkers.

The first option takes you along the south shore of Loch Sunart, through the Scottish Natural Heritage Nature Reserve. Here, work is afoot to restore the oak-woods, some of the last of the native wildwoods. This route is the easier of the two, but it is a bit longer and the view of the loch is often hidden by trees.

Your second option is to go past Glencripesdale House and walk up the Glen Cripesdale forest road before turning off on the path through the forest.

From the lochan the way down to the shore of Sunart is clear with splendid views through breaks in the forest to the north and east. The route to Laudale is along the track beside Loch Sunart, as in the first option. This second route is shorter, but steeper, improving the outlook no end.

*Philip Hinchliffe
on stone seat*

FERRY SERVICE FROM LAGA

For those who like that little extra something in their walking, the area around Cripesdale can be explored in a separate expedition by using the ferry service from Laga. This could be especially applicable if you are lodging on the north side of Loch Sunart. By prior arrangement with the ferry operator at Laga, ask to be taken across the loch to Glencripesdale House. You can reach the ferry point by leaving the A861 at Salen, to follow the B8007 along the scenic coastline for about 8km to Laga where the ferry is signed. (If you get to Glenborrodale you've gone too far.)

Once on the south shore of Sunart, you have several options. You can choose a circular walk up to Lochan Dhonnachaidh and descend by going forward down to the loch and back to Glencripesdale House to be picked up by the ferry at a prearranged time. You can walk along the loch side to Laudale, or walk back to Kinlochteacuis to be picked up there. If you do choose to use this service it is necessary to pre-book your trip, as the ferryman may have other clients. He is very flexible and willing to take you anywhere you wish. His phone number can be obtained from the TIC at Strontian.

Route notes

A   Leave the road head at 656542 and walk along the estate road through the gate. Cross the river (over the bridge), and then keep left towards Rahoy to continue on the estate road.

Barge Jetty near Cripesdale House

B   Just after the cattle grid, turn right at a point marked with a post (but no sign) and ascend the access track to the tiny cottage (Caorann). With the cottage on your left, ascend the track a few metres more until you can identify a waymark post (Scottish Rights of Way and Access Society) over by the deer fence to the right. Cross the rough grass to this point and ascend alongside the fence, following subsequent marker posts to the skyline. Going very rough. (Note This right of way – which does not follow precisely the OS marked

Map continues p.134

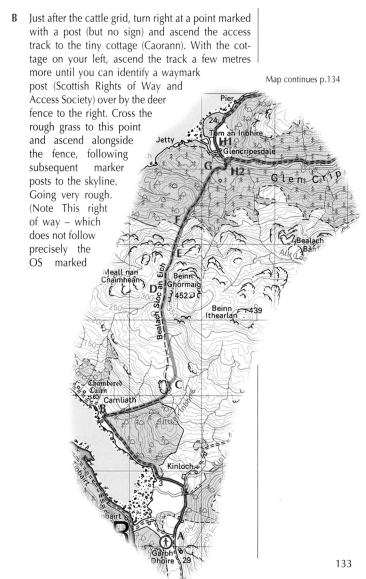

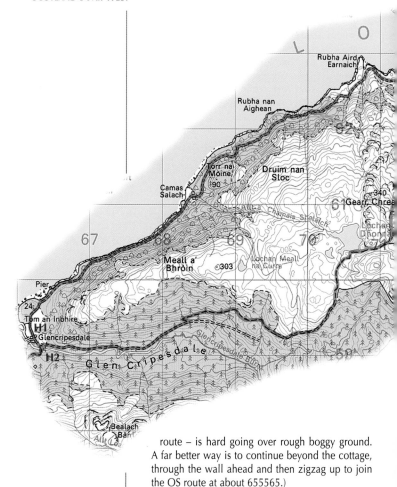

route – is hard going over rough boggy ground. A far better way is to continue beyond the cottage, through the wall ahead and then zigzag up to join the OS route at about 655565.)

C   The ground becomes less steep as you continue by the fence. At 657562, turn left away from the fence towards another marker post.

D Continue ahead across open ground to the shoulder on the left of Beinn Ghormaig. At about 655573 you should encounter another waymark. Past over Bealach Sloc an Eich, then follow more waymarks to the N. No defined path.

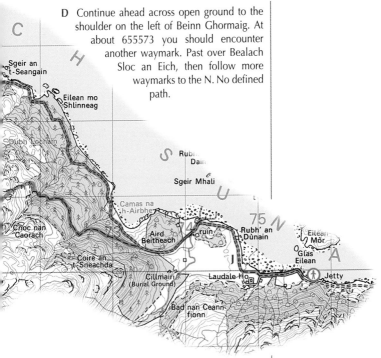

E The descent on the undefined path is waymarked. It is very, very steep and very, very rough. Do be careful.

F Enter the forest via the stile. The path through the forest is waymarked and fairly clear.

G Cross the burn via the bridge. On approaching Glencripesdale House, you need to decide whether to follow the track along the shores of Loch Sunart or to climb up Glen Cripesdale and get to the shore track at 734603.

H1 If you choose the shore track, keep ahead with Glencripesdale House visible to your right. Follow the track along the S shore of Loch Sunart. The going is quite straightforward, passing in front of Laudale House just before the end of the walk.

H2 If you choose the high-level route, turn right to Glencripesdale House and follow the forest road up the glen. At 684594, turn sharp left into a well-defined path into the forest, then turn sharp right and continue over the summit of the ridge. Keep Lochan Dhonnachaidh on your left. In places, this path is wet and difficult ...

I   The path continues to be well-defined but very wet in places. In the forest it becomes a forest road and the descent is quite clear down to the shore track.

J   Continue eastwards on the track, in front of Laudale House and to the road head at 756599.

WALK 5

Glen Gour

Start:	A861 near Sallachan, SW of Corran ferry (978626); roadside parking
Finish:	Car park in Ariundle National Nature Reserve N of Strontian (826633)
Distance:	17km (10.5 miles)
Route features:	Good track initially; then only occasional defined rough path, sometimes wet. River to ford; end of route on forest tracks
OS map:	Explorer 391 Ardgour & Strontian

This route passes along tracks, paths and sometimes through rough, boggy areas but, as the highest point is only 200m, is not physically demanding, but it is a longish walk. During the ascent make sure you look back down Glen Gour quite often, as the views are magical, particularly across Loch Linnhe.

There is limited car parking on the seaward side of the A861, near Sallachan, just over 4km southwest from the Corran ferry.

On reaching the watershed at the top of Glen Gour, you pass to the north of Lochan a' Chothruim (Lochan of the Watershed). Keeping to the north of the river the walk passes a ruined farm and enters Ariundle National Nature Reserve, a naturalist's paradise. This is a 70ha-remnant of the oak forests which once stretched along the whole of the west coast of Great Britain as far south as Devon. In the late 18th and the early 19th century, the woods on this southeast-facing slope were coppiced to provide

Down Glen Gour to Loch Linnhe

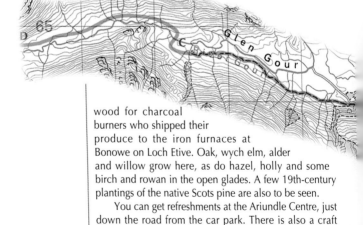

wood for charcoal
burners who shipped their
produce to the iron furnaces at
Bonowe on Loch Etive. Oak, wych elm, alder
and willow grow here, as do hazel, holly and some
birch and rowan in the open glades. A few 19th-century
plantings of the native Scots pine are also to be seen.

You can get refreshments at the Ariundle Centre, just
down the road from the car park. There is also a craft
workshop, an interpretive centre and a lochan for those
who want to try their hand at fishing.

WILDLIFE IN THE NATURE RESERVE

Mosses thrive in the reserve; over 250 different species have been identified. There are many spring flowers such as violet, primrose, wood anemone and lesser celandine. The trees, flowers and abundant grasses attract many birds. Tits, woodpeckers and owls appear the year round, to be joined in summer by willow warblers, spotted flycatchers and redstarts. There are over 40 species of moth, together with many butterflies.

Route notes

A   Walk a short distance on the road towards Corran, then turn left into the side road (probably the original road) leading to Sallachan.

B   Just before the bridge over the River Gour, pass through the gate on the left which gives access to the estate track. After about 3.5km from Sallachan, walk past a small wood and a sheepfold on the left. In due course, the track starts to descend towards the river. At 932645, take the right fork where the track bifurcates. Beware of the false right turn a few metres beforehand. The track ends after about 1km. (**Note** The Explorer OS map, current at the time of research, shows a path beyond 961635, not a track, and it is shown ending along the glen at the sheepfold.)

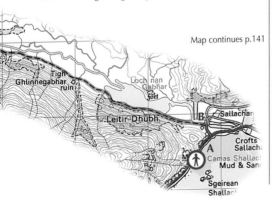

Map continues p.141

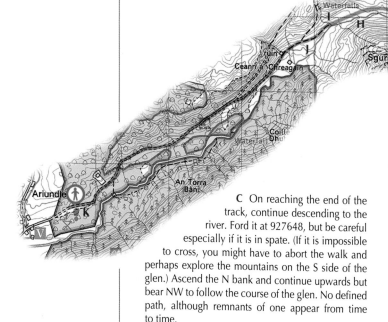

C On reaching the end of the track, continue descending to the river. Ford it at 927648, but be careful especially if it is in spate. (If it is impossible to cross, you might have to abort the walk and perhaps explore the mountains on the S side of the glen.) Ascend the N bank and continue upwards but bear NW to follow the course of the glen. No defined path, although remnants of one appear from time to time.

D The going is rough, but not difficult. The glen narrows as it approaches the gorge.

E Passing through the gorge may be the most difficult part of the whole walk. If there is little water in the river, you could walk beside it but the going is rough. The better way is to proceed on a course higher up on the N side of the glen, but it is steep so be careful, especially if there is snow and ice around.

F Keep on the N side of Lochan a' Chothruim and descend the glen. Keep to the N side of the river. There is no path, but the going is not difficult.

G Keep to the N side
of the river. No formal
path. Rough going.

H The remains of enclosures appear, together with
ruins of small buildings. Traces of a path will be
found and, as you descend the glen, it becomes more
defined.

I On approaching the forest the path becomes a track. A
gate gives access to enclosed land, and a second gate
gives access to the Ariundle National Nature Reserve.

J Ascend gently to join the forest track. Keep left and
follow it to the car park at:

K If you are being met by a vehicle your walk ends
here. If you are staying in Strontian, continue on the
metalled lane to the minor road. Then keep left and
follow this for 1.5km to the village.

WALK 6

Coire an Iubhair

Start & finish:	Near old road bridge by A861 at E end of Glen Tarbert (928597); good parking area
Distance:	7km (4.5 miles) return
Route features:	Well-defined track and path all the way; wet in places
OS map:	Explorer 391 Ardgour & Strontian

This lovely route up Coire an Iubhair is clear, and as the glen narrows at its upper reaches you become surrounded by Garbh Bheinn (885m), Beinn Bheig (658m) and Sgorr Mhic Eacharna (650m). It should be quite possible to climb any of these peaks although we have not checked the routes.

Up Choire an Iubhair

Whilst researching walks, we have occasionally been disappointed to discover that a proposed route was unsuitable. But then that is the purpose of research. Having based ourselves at Strontian for a few days, we set out to look at a walk from the A861 in Glen Tarbert. We wanted to make our way southerly over the summits of Meall a' Choirein Lurchraich (539m) – what a fine sounding name), Maol Odhar (794m), Creach Bheinn (853m) and down into Glen Galmadale. However, the best-laid plans of mice and men and so on put paid to that idea; our way was blocked by a deer fence with a locked gate, and we had to abort the project. But all was not lost. We decided to explore Coire an Iubhair, which we discovered was a delightful glen in which to enjoy an afternoon's stroll. There is a lovely bubbling river with the occasional tree, a defined path and even a parking place for several cars.

Route notes

A   Start at the parking place near to the bridge on the old road at 928597. Cross the old road into the well-defined path.

B   Follow this path to join the main track at the gate and stile. Follow the track into the glen.

C   The track degenerates to a path, which is well defined and wet in places.

D   The path peters out, so you could stop and return, or continue on the rough ground until time runs out. Return by the same route.

WALK 7

Meall a' Chuilinn

Start & finish:	Limited Forest Enterprise parking area on A861 in Glen Tarbert east of Strontian (867605)
Distance:	9km (5.6 miles) return
Route features:	Forest road, followed by wet and boggy pathless way along forest fence and up to summit
OS map:	Explorer 391 Ardgour & Strontian

If you turn west into Glen Tarbert on the A861 from the Corran ferry, you cannot fail to be impressed by the pre-eminent bulk of Garb Bheinn (885m), the second highest mountain in Ardgour. From its summit there is a magnificent overview of Glen Tarbert and Loch Linnhe, and it can be climbed from Coire an Iubhair (see Walk 6). However, nearer to the A861 and lower than Garb Bheinn lies Meall a' Chuilinn (687m), the ascent of which will present you with a pleasant surprise.

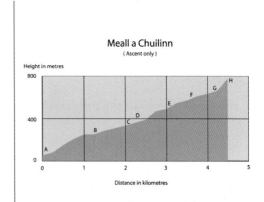

144

Meall a' Chuilinn cairn

There is room for a couple of cars, without blocking the forest entrance gate, at 867605 about 6km east of Strontian. Forest Enterprise signs and maps mark the spot.

The way along the forest road zigzagging up the hillside is easy and uneventful (**A**). There is no path along the forest fence to the east (**C**) and it can be quite wet and boggy when crossing the many gullies. The surprise comes at point **D** where you will encounter a great wide rift in the mountainside, heading almost due north, many metres deep, with the Allt a' Chait flowing south in the bottom. We can find no explanation for this geological phenomenon in any of many reference books, and can only assume that it may be due to water erosion over a long period. What is even more surprising is that the fissure turns sharp right towards its upper end (**E**) before it diminishes in width and depth.

From the lochan at **G**, a short walk to the southeast will reveal Glen Tarbert almost in its entirety as well as magnificent views over Loch Linnhe. An easy scramble northwards up the steep slope from the lochan brings you to the summit ridge where there are fine views over Ardgour to the north. ▶

We have offered a variation on the return route from **D** (see box p147). Be prepared for many deviations amongst tussocky grass and dodgings through the new forestry plantation as you return to your vehicle.

Route notes

A   At the entrance to the forest, cross the stile to the right of the gate and follow the forest road as it zigzags up and over the summit of the ridge.

145

*View from top of
Meall a' Chuilinn*

B A few hundred metres before the bridge over the burn, cross the stile next to the gate giving access to the open moor. Turn right.

C Outside the forest area, follow the fence along its course keeping it on your right for about 1km, until a stile is encountered. No path. (This stile gives access back to the forest area. **Note** At the time of research the forest boundary on the ground, and as depicted on the Forestry map posted at **A**, differs from that shown

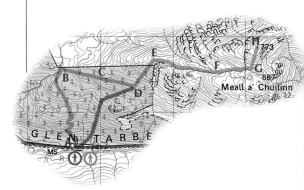

on OS Explorer 391. This map shows this boundary running as a straight line from **B** to **E**. Earlier OS maps show older forest boundaries.)

D Leave the stile and the forest area to ascend steeply, slightly E of N. No path. To the right is a very deep gully, so keep well away from its edge.

E Follow the gully as it turns E, keeping to its north side. In due course the gully is less precipitous and can be entered to continue upwards until it peters out.

F On leaving the gully keep slightly N of E for a few hundred metres among the broken ground, until a lochan is reached.

G The area around the lochan is well worth exploring, and a few hundred metres to its SE there is a magnificent panoramic view over Glen Tarbert and Loch Linnhe and fine views of Garbh Bheinn.

An ascent northwards up the steep slope from the lochan enables you to reach the summit ridge at **H**, from which there is a vast panorama northwards including Sgurr Dhomhnuill.

Return by the ascent route.

VARIANT ROUTE FROM D

Cross the stile into the forest area and descend generally southwestwards to A. This is a very difficult way over rough ground amongst young trees. Also **A** is not initially visible, so direction finding is not easy, but it is much shorter than following the ascent route.

WALK 8

Sgurr Dhomhnuill

Start & finish:	Car park in Ariundle National Nature Reserve N of Strontian (826633)
Distance:	17km (10.5 miles) return
Route features:	Good track/path to old mine; then pathless rough and boggy until steep and rough scramble to summit
OS map:	Explorer 391 Ardgour & Strontian

If you have studied the walk along the Druim Garbh ridge you will recollect that it stopped short of ascending Sgurr Dhomhnuill (Donald's Rocky Peak), at 888m the highest mountain in Ardgour. These notes describe the ascent of this fine peak, starting from the Ariundle National Nature Reserve.

To reach the starting point, take the Strontian to Polloch road going north from the A861 from the west side of the bridge crossing the Strontian River. After about 1.5km fork right into the well-signed forest road. The car park is less than 1km from this fork.

The first part of the walk through Strontian Glen along a well-defined path is very pleasant and easy. On arriving at the dismantled, early 18th-century Old Bellsgrove mine (**D**) (not to be confused with the 'Bellsgrove mine' which is near the Strontian to Polloch road), the path disappears altogether and your navigational abilities will come into full play. The going becomes rough, and boggy in places, ascending all the time.

At **F**, the route goes along the north flank of Sgurr na h-Ighinn to the bealach at 888673, but it is interesting to note that old maps show a route over the ridge. At one time there was a path (perhaps a rudimentary one) linking Sgurr nan Cnamh across Glen Gour, Sgurr a' Chaorainn,

Sgurr Dhomhnuill, Druim Garbh and Beinn Mheadhoin. That would be the ultimate ridge walk in Ardgour, but beyond the scope of the average walker.

Having arrived at the bealach it is a short, steep scramble to reach the summit of Sgurr Dhomhnuill. It gets easier the higher you go. The view from the top is magnificent in all directions.

Return by the same route.

ALTERNATIVE ROUTE

There is an **alternative return route** via Druim Garbh to the highest point of the Strontian to Polloch road (see Walk 9), but this should only be attempted by very fit and experienced mountain walkers.

Route notes

A Leave the car park, walking on the forest road, which degenerates to a rough track.

B At the fork keep left ascending gently.

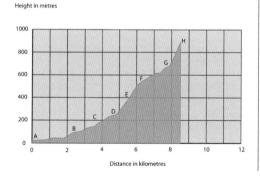

Sgurr Dhomhnuill (Walk 8)
(Ascent only)

Height in metres

Distance in kilometres

C Leave the forest through the gate and continue on the path.

D At the disused lead mines take the path to the right and cross the spoil heaps. Continue forward over the mound to find a footbridge over the burn. This footbridge is in a poor state, so take care in crossing.

E Ascend the broad ridge, no formal path. The going is very rough but keep generally ascending.

F Here, at 880669, keep to the left to discontinue ascending the ridge. A way is discernible on the north side of Sgurr na h-Ighinn which looks like a path but is a natural formation. (You could, of course, keep to the ridge over Sgurr na h-Ighinn, but we have not researched this route).

G Ascend to the bealach at 888672. Turn north to scramble up the S ridge of Sgurr Dhomhnuill. The going is steep and rough but not difficult or dangerous.

H From the summit there are fine panoramas in all directions.

Return by the same route.

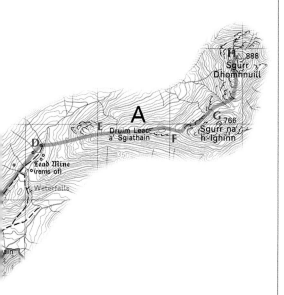

If you are a very fit and experienced mountain walker you could combine this walk with the Druim Garbh walk (Walk 9) to make a horseshoe, and either way round would make a fine expedition. This would entail crossing the bealach at 886681, joining the summit of Sgurr Dhomhnuill (**H** on this walk) with that at 882684 (**D** on Walk 9). A steep scramble down and then up is necessary. We have not researched this crossing.

WALK 9

Druim Garbh Ridge

Start & finish: Roadside parking on Strontian to Pollach road (838665)
Distance: 11km (6.8 miles) return
Route features: No paths and no direct route; wet in places
OS map: Explorer 391 Ardgour & Strontian

The highest point of the Strontian to Polloch road (364m) lies on a ridge, joining Beinn Resipol (845m) in the west with Sgurr Dhomhnuill (888m) in the east. This walk takes you east along the ridge to visit Druim Garbh, stopping short of Sgurr Dhomhnuill.

To reach the starting point, take the road from Strontian to Polloch, leaving the A861 on the west side of the bridge over the Strontian River to proceed north. Follow the road through Scotstown and Ariundle and past the mine

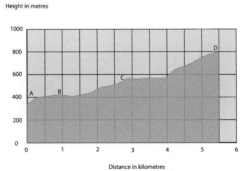

Druim Garbh Ridge (Walk 9)
(Ascent only)

152

SGURR DHOMHNUILL

From the cairn marking the end of the Druim Garbh ridge, you can see the imposing bulk of Sgurr Dhomhnuill. A descent to the col and a scramble up to the summit is possible for experienced mountain walkers, but we have not researched this route (see Walk 8 for an alternative ascent).

workings to the highest point. Here you will discover a small radio mast with its associated equipment cabin. There is room for several vehicles to be parked nearby.

The pathless route may stretch your navigational abilities slightly as you have to find your way around several lochans and many knolls. The many false summits hide the cairn marking the end of the ridge until the last hundred metres or so.

Route notes

A   Leave the road at its highest point, near the small radio mast, and walk E to ascend a low ridge. A high point with a trig point becomes visible when the ridge starts to descend.

View from Druim Garbh to Sgurr Dhomhnuill

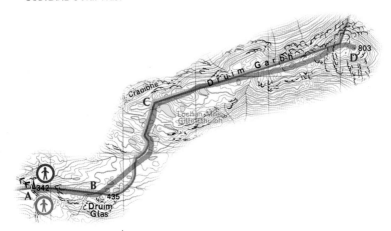

B Turn NE and skirt the head of the small valley. Continue generally NE and enter an area of lochans and knolls. Words cannot describe the route – just wend your way amongst them, proceeding generally NNE.

C Ascend the main ridge. No path, no direct route; keep ENE amongst the many false summits and lochans.

D A cairn marks the highest point of the ridge and the return point of the walk. Beyond, there is a steep descent to the col between Druim Garbh and Sgurr Dhomhnuill.

Return by the same route.

WALK 10

Beinn Resipol from Ben View Hotel

Start & finish:	Ben View Hotel, W of Strontian (801615); hotel car park by permission
Alternative finish:	A861 near Resipole – see Walk 12 (725638)
Distance:	17km (10.6 miles) return
Route features:	Lane, track and path to bealach, then pathless ascent across rough ground to summit
OS map:	Explorers 390 Ardnamurchan (East Sheet), 391 Ardgour & Strontian

Part of this walk follows an old coffin route to an ancient burial site on St Finan's Isle on Loch Shiel. Now marked by the ruins of a 16th-century chapel, it was originally a holy sanctuary established by St Finan who came over from Ireland to preach the gospel; he died in AD575.

The Ben View Hotel is well signed on the western outskirts of Strontian. Seek the owner's permission to park in

Walkers on Resipol summit

the hotel car park. The walk to Bealach nan Carn (**C**), a gentle ascent, follows one of the old coffin routes. These were used by families as highways, identified by cairns, over which to carry coffins to St Finan's Isle. From the bealach the coffin route descends to Loch Doilet and the path to the summit disappears on the open ground, becoming quite steep in places. The many false summits make the arrival at the *real* summit all the more exciting.

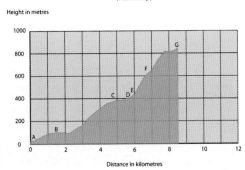

Route notes

A Follow the lane upwards. It degenerates into a track. Pass through the gate to the open moor. The track degenerates into a path.

B Turn left to ascend to the track which gives access to the Strontian waterworks. Continue ascending on the path.

C At 796654, just beyond the highest point of the path at Bealach nan Carn, turn left to leave the path. You may notice iron gateposts which, presumably,

Beinn Resipol from Ben View Hotel (Walk 10)

(Ascent only)

Height in metres

[graph: height in metres (y-axis, 0 to 1000) vs distance in kilometres (x-axis, 0 to 12), with points labelled A, B, C, D, E, F, G along the ascent profile]

Distance in kilometres

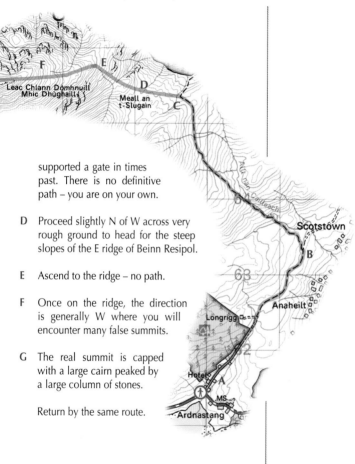

supported a gate in times past. There is no definitive path – you are on your own.

D Proceed slightly N of W across very rough ground to head for the steep slopes of the E ridge of Beinn Resipol.

E Ascend to the ridge – no path.

F Once on the ridge, the direction is generally W where you will encounter many false summits.

G The real summit is capped with a large cairn peaked by a large column of stones.

Return by the same route.

ALTERNATIVE DESCENT

Via the reverse ascent or descent described in Walk 12, in which case the distance walked will be different. Also you will have to arrange a pick-up or make your way back by road to the Ben View Hotel.

WALK 11

Doilet from Ben View Hotel

Start:	Ben View Hotel, W of Strontian (801615); hotel car park by permission
Finish:	Loch Doilet, S of Polloch (795680); roadside parking
Distance:	8.5km (5.3 miles)
Route features:	Lane, track and path (sometimes ill defined) until river, where pathless; then well-defined path through forest to road
OS map:	Explorers 390 Ardnamurchan (East Sheet), 391 Ardgour & Strontian

This walk follows the coffin route from Bealach nan Carn to Loch Doilet. From the bealach, the route passes near St Finan's Well (798655), for hundreds of years a welcome source of refreshment for weary travellers.

The Ben View Hotel is well signed on the western outskirts of Strontian; seek the owner's permission to park in the car park. The walk ascends to Bealach nan Carn (see Walk 10). Continuing downhill towards Loch Doilet, the path passes the remains of the Corrantee mine.

CORRANTEE MINE

If you decide to explore the old mine workings be careful, as they can be dangerous. This is one of about half a dozen lead mines in the Strontian area which, during their heyday in the mid 18th century, produced an annual output believed to be in the order of 600 tonnes; not a lot, but enough to keep many men employed for many years. Towards the end of the 18th century the mine owners ran into severe technical and financial difficulties which, despite the discovery of Strontianite, eventually led to the closing of the mine.

Doilet from Ben View Hotel (Walk 11)

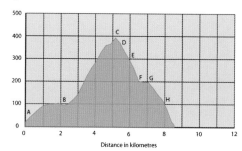

Height in metres

Distance in kilometres

Having passed the mine, the path peters out in the valley bottom where the wide river is crossed and recrossed many times. The way through the forest becomes well defined, descending steeply to the road.

Route notes

A   Follow the lane upwards. It degenerates into a track. Pass through the gate to the open moor. The track degenerates into a path.

B   Turn left to ascend to the track that gives access to the Strontian waterworks. Continue ascending on the path.

C   Continue from the bealach, descending on the well-defined path.

D   Use the ladder stile (broken at the time of research) to enter the forest. Continue descending as the path becomes less well defined.

E   Keep the disused mine workings on your right and descend to more mine workings, which you should keep on your left.

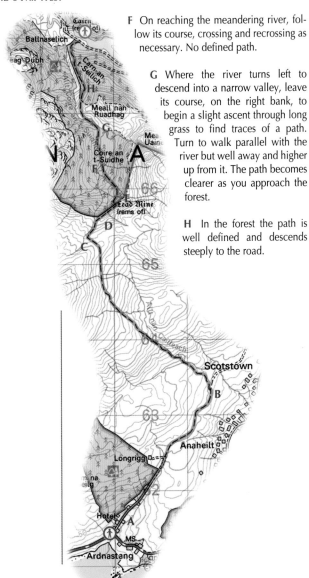

F On reaching the meandering river, follow its course, crossing and recrossing as necessary. No defined path.

G Where the river turns left to descend into a narrow valley, leave its course, on the right bank, to begin a slight ascent through long grass to find traces of a path. Turn to walk parallel with the river but well away and higher up from it. The path becomes clearer as you approach the forest.

H In the forest the path is well defined and descends steeply to the road.

WALK 12

Beinn Resipol from Resipole

Start:	A861 near Resipole, Loch Sunart (725638); roadside parking
Finish:	A861, Loch Sunart (754616); roadside parking (Forest Enterprise car park 1km W on A861 if preferred)
Distance:	11km (6.8 miles)
Route features:	Well-defined path nearly all the way up; short scramble to summit; no path on descent until Ardery
OS map:	Explorer 390 Ardnamurchan (East Sheet)

A sea level to sea level walk that avoids the false summits encountered on Walk 10.

This walk, from Resipole to Beinn Resipol (spelt differently), starts at sea level. You can park beside Loch Sunart near the drive up to the farm and walk past the campsite towards Strontian to the field gate on your left. The way up is well defined until the final slopes below the

View to Resipol summit

Beinn Resipol from Resipole   (Walk 12)

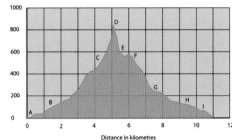

summit. We have left the last part of the ascent to your personal choice, but to avoid most of the steep scramble to the top keep the summit on your right and make a final approach from the north.

Route notes

A   Some 150m E of the campsite on the A861, a gate gives access to the hills. Pass through the gate and follow the well-defined path/track.

B   The path remains well defined, but is very rough and wet in places as it follows Alt Mhic Chiarain up the glen.

C   On approaching the steep slopes below the summit of Beinn Resipol the path becomes ill defined. The final climb is a short scramble.

D   Retrace your steps from the summit to about 761654, then strike S locating the W end of Lochan Bac an Lochain.

E   There is no defined path and the terrain is rough among rocky outcrops.

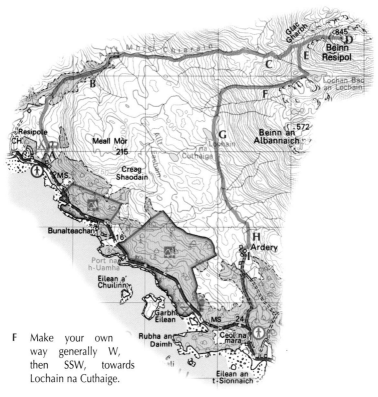

F Make your own way generally W, then SSW, towards Lochain na Cuthaige.

G Turn S, then slightly E of S, making for the makeshift bridge at 753629.

H Keep the fence on your right as far as the gate at 754628, to gain access to the enclosed land around Ardery.

I A track is now clear and descends in front of the house away to the left. Walk through the woods and, after passing through the gate in the deer fence, down to the A861 at 754616.

Walks based on Salen

WALK 13

Acharacle to Glenborrodale

Start:	Acharacle, N of Salen A861 (675681); roadside parking near school
Finish:	Glenborrodale, B8007 (607608); roadside parking
Distance:	12km (7.5 miles)
Route features:	Well-defined track and paths all the way
OS map:	Explorer 390 Ardnamurchan (East Sheet)

The village of Glenborrodale is home to the RSPB's most westerly nature reserve on the British mainland. It has a nature trail that takes you through delightful woodland and moorland. Some 3 or 4km along the coast to the west is the Ardnamurchan Natural History Centre, which is also well worth a visit.

Acharacle to Glenborrodale (Walk 13)

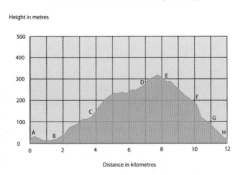

Acharacle (pronounced 'Akaar-akle') is on the A861, about 4km north of Salen. There is space to park your vehicle in the lane near the school; be mindful of the comings and goings of parents and children.

After the left turn at **B**, the way ascends gently past a sheepfold and waterworks to Loch Laga (**C**) with its distinctive boathouse. On the ascent, keep looking back to the north for views of Kentra Bay and Castle Tioram, and to the northwest for the isles of Muck, Eigg and

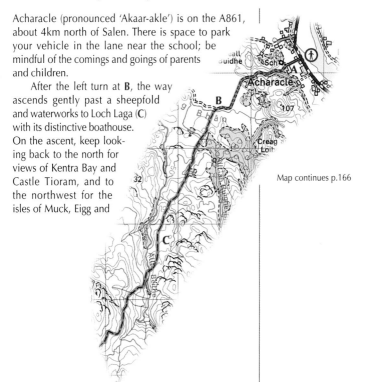

Map continues p.166

Rum. Across the loch lies the bulk of Ben Laga (512m). Indeed, if you are feeling particularly fit, you may be inclined to take the (ill-defined) left fork at the end of the loch (**D**) and make the return trip ascent to the summit. Due to its many false summits, this ascent may take longer than you think, and if you want to save it until later see Walk 14.

From the tranquil dark waters of the loch, the route climbs slightly and then it's all downhill to Glenborrodale on the B8007 coast road. Glenborrodale Castle, with its late Victorian castellated towers, is now a hotel.

Route notes

A   Beyond the school, away from the A861, the lane degenerates into a track. Ascend and follow the track over the rise and then descend to open level ground.

B   Turn left at the junction of tracks and cross the burn. Continue on this track, which degenerates into a path beyond a waterworks.

C   The path is well defined all the way to Loch Laga, with its boathouse on your left.

D   Ignore the left fork (ill defined, which descends to Laga Bay) and keep ahead on the gently ascending well-defined path.

E   Descend gently, crossing the burn at the broken bridge.

F   At the T-junction turn left and descend to the forest. Continue descending on the edge of the forest.

G   Keep left.

H   The track bifurcates. Either route gets you to the B8007.

WALK 14

Ben Laga

Start & finish:	Laga, W of Salen, B8007 (633612); roadside parking
Alternative finish:	Glenborrodale, B8007 (607609)
Distance:	4.5km (2.8 miles) return
Route features:	Track and path, sometimes ill defined, until ascent of W face where pathless to summit
OS map:	Explorer 390 Ardnamurchan (East Sheet)

This is the shortest way to the top of Ben Laga (512m), from where there are good views over Loch Sunart into Morvern.

Take the B8007 coast road west from Salen and find a suitable parking place in Laga, just before Glenborrodale.

From Ben Laga summit to Loch Sunart

Ben Laga (Walk 14)

(Ascent only)

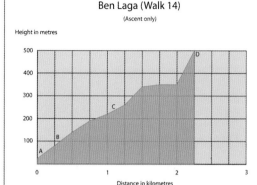

The way to the summit area (**A–C**) is fairly straightforward, but locating the trig point amongst the false summits may entertain you for more than a few minutes.

You can return by the same route, or make your way to join up with Walk 13 at **D**, returning to Glenborrodale. You will then have a walk of about 3km easterly along the B8007 to rejoin your vehicle.

Route notes

A   Leave the B8007 up the track situated 100m NE of the bridge (633611) over the Allt Mór at Laga. Keep ascending the track, which becomes a path on leaving the enclosed land.

B   The path, undefined in places, zigzags upwards.

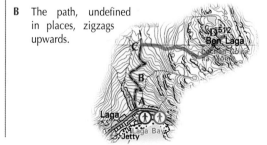

C   The path becomes well defined. Some 200m along this defined stretch, leave it to ascend E up the W face of the Ben. No path, but grassy slopes afford routes to the summit ridge.

Summit cairn on Ben Laga

D   The summit trig point is not immediately apparent, but it is not difficult to find. The route, amongst false summits, is generally NE.

Return by the same route.

ALTERNATIVE DESCENT

Follow the same route to reach the level ground at point C. Ascend the path (N) to join the Acharacle to Glenborrodale route at D, close to Loch Laga. Turn left and follow this route to Glenborrodale.

WALK 15

Blain Circular

Start & finish:	Blain, near Shiel Bridge, N of Acharacle, A861 (675692); roadside parking
Distance:	9.5km (5.9 miles); short cut 6km (3.7 miles)
Route features:	Tracks and paths, sometimes rough and wet
OS map:	Explorer 390 Ardnamurchan (East Sheet)

There are at least two Shiel Bridges – and one Bridge of Shiel – in the Highlands of Scotland. The one relevant to locating the start of this walk is the Shiel Bridge just north of Archaracle at the seaward end of Loch Shiel. The walk is, in general, uncomplicated on tracks, paths and some sections of road.

Before embarking on this circular walk – the only one in Moidart, and which includes magnificent views out to sea – you can park your vehicle near Blain Farm, currently a bungalow, on the bend of the road at 676693.

Having negotiated the lochans above Blain, the path continues to rise until a rough, wet descent brings you to the cairn (**K**). A further descent brings you to the path along the shore of Loch Moidart. This path was cut into the rocky hillside some 130 years ago, and some sections have eroded and care is required. The way along here is known as the Silver Walk since, in the 19th century, a cache of Elizabethan coins was discovered near Castle Tioram. It is just possible, too, that the hoard was first stolen from the castle in the 17th century.

If you take the short cut (Variant 1), you will pass by Clanranald's Seat (668712), a boulder from which Clanranald is said to have watched the huge pall of smoke arising from the funeral pyre of his beloved Tioram.

CASTLE TIORAM

The 14th-century Castle Tioram, built on the site of a previous fortress and the stronghold of the MacDonalds of Clanranald for some five centuries, is now in ruins. This great Highland family ruled land and sea and Tioram, whilst being attacked on many occasions, was never taken. Tradition has it that the castle was put to the torch in 1715 and destroyed by the clan chief himself, to prevent it falling into English hands while he was absent.

This derelict fortress has recently been the subject of intense debate in Scotland. The present owner, with the support of the current clan chief, wishes to restore it to its original magnificence and use it as his residence, albeit with public access. Other factions want the castle to maintain its historical fabric. The debate continues but we hope that this splendid edifice will remain as a reminder of the clan tradition.

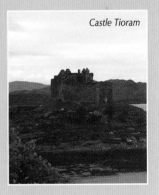

Castle Tioram

Tioram (pronounced 'Cheerum') is usually accessible (M), but do be careful as the tide can come in very quickly, making retreat to the mainland impossible.

Route notes

A   Access to the hills from the road is at the gate by the bend in the road (676693). Walk through the gap beside the gate to the track.

B   Follow the track and pass through the stile at the next gate.

C   On leaving the wooded area the track bends right. Keep to the track. Do NOT be tempted by the path off to the left.

D   Some 100m beyond the wood the track bifurcates. Take the left fork and keep ahead (N).

E The track degenerates into a very rough path. Keep ascending.

F At the head of Loch Blain (on your left), bend left (W) to cross the small dam of the next lochan (two stiles).

G Turn to keep this lochan on your right.

H At the isolated hawthorn bush the path bifurcates (see Variant 1). Turn sharp right, continuing to ascend.

I The path remains well-defined but quite rough and wet in places.

J The descent is rough and wet.

K A cairn marks the junction of paths (see Variant 2). Turn sharp left to descend to the shore.

L Continue on the well-defined path on the side of the sea loch. The going is very rough and precarious in places. No ambiguity as to the route.

M The way opens out to a grassy area, with Castle Tioram accessible provided the tide is not too high.

N Walk along the sand, keeping the fence on your left. At the car park, join the public road for a few metres then keep right into the private road.

O Walk along this private road until it meets the public road, then continue to its junction with the main road (A861). Turn left to get back to the starting point.

VARIANT 1: A SHORT CUT

Instead of turning right at the hawthorn bush (**H**), continue ahead to ascend. Beyond the summit, continue on the N side of a lochan. The path is not very clear. However beyond the dam the path becomes defined and descends beside an iron water pipe. On reaching a field, continue forwards to the stile and into the public road. Turn left and continue to the main road (A861) and the starting point.

VARIANT 2: TOWARDS LOCH MOIDART

Instead of turning sharp left at the cairn (**K**), continue ahead on the defined path, which eventually ascends in a small gorge. Rough going. Beyond the highest point of the gorge, the path degenerates and becomes difficult. It terminates at the ruins of a croft, from which can be seen the head of Loch Moidart, although trees may obscure the view to some extent. Return to the main route.

Loch Blain

WALK 16

Kentra Bay to Ockle – the 'Singing Sands'

Start:	Arivegaig, off B8044 W of Acharacle (650677); roadside parking
Finish:	Ockle (556704); off-road parking
Distance:	11.5km (7.1 miles)
Route features:	Tracks and paths all the way
OS map:	Explorer 390 Ardnamurchan (East & West Sheets)

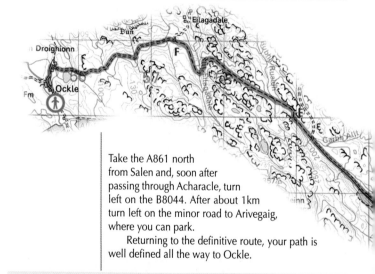

Take the A861 north
from Salen and, soon after
passing through Acharacle, turn
left on the B8044. After about 1km
turn left on the minor road to Arivegaig,
where you can park.

Returning to the definitive route, your path is
well defined all the way to Ockle.

Crofters used this path between Acharacle and Ockle as a vital route
for hundreds of years. It joined many small communities, scattered far
and wide, along the stark wind- and storm-swept northern coast
of Ardnamurchan.

BURIED VILLAGE

A diversion of a few hundred metres to visit the beach at **C** is well worthwhile. Camas an Lighe (the Beach of Flooding), is so-called because hundreds of years ago a village became buried, or 'flooded', by the ever-shifting, pure white, 'singing' sands; the sands 'sing' as you walk across them. It is said that brooches and kilt pins are sometimes dredged up from the depths of the sands, supporting the legend that a battle was fought in this magical place during the '45 Jacobite Rising.

Route notes

A Begin at the end of a minor road (650677), leading from the B8044 to access Arivegaig. Pass through the gate and over the bridge to continue on the well-defined track that follows the shore of Kentra Bay.

B Ford the burn, keeping Gorteneorn away to your left. About 200m beyond the house the well-defined track leaves the sea and enters a forest.

C (**Note** It is worthwhile descending this track to the right to explore the beautiful sands at Camus an Lighe). The **definitive route** continues on the main track and leaves the forest.

D Soon after leaving the forest fork left to join the path which leads up the brae.

E The path is well defined all the way. Pass over the summit of the brae and descend on the path.

F Join the track and turn left to continue all the way to Ockle.

WALK 17

Fascadale to the Lighthouse

Start:	Fascadale (501707); roadside parking
Finish:	Lighthouse on Point of Ardnamurchan (416675); visitor car park
Distance:	15km (9.3 miles)
Route features:	Tracks and paths (mix of defined and ill defined)
OS map:	Explorer 390 Ardnamurchan (West Sheet)

Due to the very craggy nature of the northern coast of Ardnamurchan, this walk does not follow the coastline but bears inland across moorland.

From Salen take the B8007 coast road through Laga and Glenborrodale. After passing Loch Mudle on your right, take the right turn at the T-junction and keep straight ahead to the tiny hamlet of Fascadale where you will be able to park your vehicle off-road.

After passing through the fascinating deserted village of Glendrian (**G**), a short walk down the road will bring you to Achnaha (**J**). This whole area has particular significance to geologists because it is a huge ring dyke, resulting from furious volcanic activity millions of years ago. The vast caldera – which is perhaps only evident to the trained eye but is discernible on the OS Explorer map – encircles Glen Drian (the Glen of the Hawthorns) and

POINT OF ARDNAMURCHAN

The lonely Point of Ardnamurchan is the most westerly point of the British mainland. The point has a lighthouse built of Mull granite, a small tearoom and a museum. Since automation in 1988 it is not possible to visit the tower itself.

View towards Portuairk

the village of Achnaha. From here the way to the beautiful bay of Portuairk (**O**), though somewhat convoluted, is not too difficult to follow.

Route notes

A Leave the lane on the well-defined broad track. After 200m or so it descends to a burn. Cross, and ascend the rough ground SW. No defined path.

B No defined path, but keep generally N of W with Lochan Dubh on your left. Rough and wet.

C A defined path becomes visible, descending steadily.

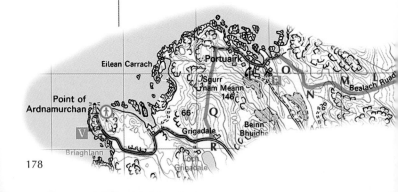

D Keep left at this junction. (If you wish, you could descend 400m or so down to the sea by turning right.)

E The path proceeds SW, then S, then SE into a small gorge, where the path is very wet in places.

F The path turns S, is defined, then turns SE to pass the ruins at Glendrian.

G The well-defined path descends to the burn and then ascends.

H The path is well-defined, ascending steadily. Pass through the stile and down to the lane.

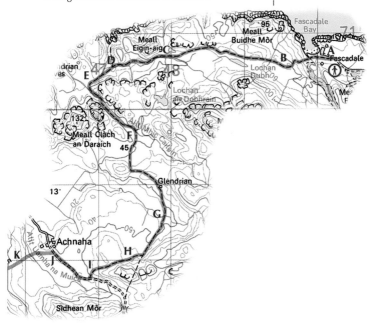

I   Turn right at the lane and proceed to Achnaha.

J   Just before the house on the left, leave the lane beside the fence and follow this fence to open ground. Turn SW – no visible path.

K   Begin the ascent. A line of posts marking the route becomes visible.

L   Continue over the summit of the bealach and descend on the well-defined path. Lower down, at a point where the path crosses the burn, leave the path and go right, across rough terrain to join the grassy path visible about 100m away.

Foghorn and lighthouse at Point of Ardnamurchan

M Continue descending on the reasonably defined path, recrossing the burn. At a point roughly between two electrical transmission posts (the right of which has an 'isolator switch') leave the path and aim right for yet another crossing of the burn, marked by a scar on its far bank.

N Continue on the fairly well defined path. Aim to pass beneath the rocky outcrop (on your right), on a reasonably defined path through bracken. Walk towards the birch wood with a fence on your left on the other side of the burn. Cross the iron bridge over the burn and ascend, crossing the stile and into the wood. On leaving the wood, the way opens out into bracken and lilies. Follow the fairly well-defined path towards the coast.

O Pass the two concrete (marker?) posts and descend to the fence and the reeds. Keep the fence on your left and cross the stile. Keep ahead to the sandy cove and cross the footbridges. Walk along the path and lane to the T-junction in the village of Portuairk

P Turn right, then continue on the lane through the village towards the sea. At its end, a gate gives access to open ground. After several metres the way becomes unclear, but ascend W on an ill-defined path. At about the highest point on this path, turn left to proceed S on open ground.

Q Beyond the summit of the bealach, a house and the lane to the lighthouse become visible. Descend, passing through a gate into enclosed land towards the house (Grigadale). Pass between the house and an outbuilding to the drive, and then through a gate into the lane.

R Turn right on the lane and follow it all the way to the lighthouse.

WALK 18

Ben Hiant

Start & finish:	B8007 S of Loch Mudle (544653); in roadside excavation
Distance:	6km (3.7 miles)
Route features:	Rough going along pathless boggy moorland; steep scramble to the summit. After ridge, only occasional signs of paths
OS map:	Explorer 390 Ardnamurchan (West Sheet)

At 528m Ben Hiant – the Holy Mountain – is Ardnamurchan's highest point. It is not clear why it is so called, but it is thought that St Columba may have passed this way on one of his trips. Beinn Resipol, in Sunart, is higher, but in our opinion the views to Mull and over the peninsula are more spectacular from Hiant. It may help you to identify the surrounding countryside and the many islands if you have a small-scale map with you.

From Salen, follow the B8007 coast road through Glenborrodale and Glenmore. The road then turns inland at

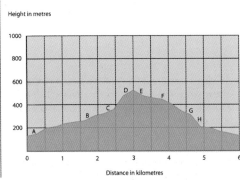

Ben Hiant   (Walk 18)

Denis Brook and Ben Hiant

Ardslignish (where there is a viewing point to Loch Sunart) to pass to the east of Ben Hiant. Just to the south of Loch Mudle (ahead), look out for a parking area in an old sandpit on your left.

Once on foot from the parking spot, it can be quite rough going across boggy moorland with little signs of paths (**A/B**). The ascent from the bealach (**C**) becomes almost an uphill scramble, but the reward on reaching the summit cairn at **D** makes it all worthwhile.

On a clear day you will have uninterrupted views over the whole peninsula and many, many islands.

The descent is straightforward, as you can see the parking area ahead.

Route notes

A   Climb the bank from the parking place to the open moor. You will see the main summit half-right. Proceed towards it SSW on a faint path which soon disappears.

B   Undulating ground – no path. Turn SW towards the bealach between Beinn na h-Urchrach and Ben Hiant. Rough going, but not difficult.

C At the bealach, turn S to ascend a grassy incline which becomes a broad gully with scree. It is very steep higher up and becomes almost a scramble.

D On reaching the top of the gully, turn left (E) to access the summit with its trig point and cairn. Looking NE from the summit you will see a well-defined path along the NE ridge.

E To access this path for your descent, retrace your steps a few metres. Descend SE, then E, to circuit round the summit mound on a rather precarious steep slope. The path becomes clearer, but rough.

F On leaving the summit mound, follow the well-defined path along and down the ridge.

G At 545638, the path fizzles out. Turn N, and 20m ahead, at 545640, a small cairn is encountered.

H Continue due N to the parking place, deviating only to negotiate steep slopes.

BIBLIOGRAPHY

Of the many reference and other books used during the preparation of this guide, the authors would, in particular, like to record the following:

Adam, J. S. Gaelic Wordbook (Chambers, 1995)

Angus, S. et al. *AA/OS Scottish Highlands Guide* (AA/OS, 1994)

Bartholomew, J. (Ed) *Scottish Hill Tracks* (Scottish Rights of Way Society, 1995)

Bennet, D. *The Munros* (Scottish Mountaineering Club, 1985)

Brook, D. & Hinchliffe, P. *North to the Cape* (Cicerone, 1999)

Brown, O. & Whittaker, J. *Walking in North Mull* (Brown & Whittaker, 2002)*

Brown O. & Whittaker J. *Walking in South Mull & Iona* (Brown & Whittaker, 1996)*

Clapham, F. M. (ed) *A Factbook of British History* (Rainbow Books, 1993)

French, D. (ed) *The Rambler's Year Book & Accommodation Guide* (The Rambler's Association, 2003)

Gunn, G. & Spankie, M. *The Highland Clearances* (Wayland Publishers Ltd, 1993)

Haswell-Smith, H. *The Scottish Islands* (Canongate, 2001)

Howard, J. and Jones, A. *The Isle of Ulva* (private, 1990)

James, C. *Torosay Castle & Gardens* (Pillings Printing Co Ltd, no date)

Johnston, S. et al. *The Corbetts and Other Scottish Hills* (Scottish Mountaineering Club, 1996)

Maclean, C. *The Isle of Mull* (Maclean Publications, 1997)

Maclean, L. *Duart Castle* (Jarrold Publishing, 2000)

Macnab, P. A. *Mull & Iona* (Pevensey Press, 2001)

Murray, W. H. *The Companion Guide to The West Highlands of Scotland* (Collins, 1968)

Wightman, A. *Who Owns Scotland* (Canongate Books, 1996)

Whittaker J. *Mull: Monuments and History* (Brown & Whittaker, 1999)*

Whittaker J. *Mull: Natural History* (Brown & Whittaker, 1995)*

* The series of books by Olive Brown and Jean Whittaker proved to be particularly useful to us during our research.

The dates given are those of the editions consulted. In addition, many town and village guides, tourist guides and brochures were read. Our appreciation goes to all the (often anonymous) authors and publishers who compiled them.

APPENDIX 1

Place Names

Many place names in Scotland's Far West are derived from Gaelic or Norse origins. Here are a few words and meanings, which may help with your map reading. The terms in parentheses represent the Anglicised pronunciation.

Aber	Mouth or confluence of a river	Inbhir (*inver*)	Confluence of waters
Abhainn	River	Kin	Head
Achadh (*achug*)	Field	Kirk	Church
Airidh	Shieling	Kyle	Narrow strait of water
Allt	Stream, water		
Aonach (*aynach*)	Ridge	Lagan	Little hollow
Ard	High, lofty	Liathe	Grey
Ban	White	Linne	Pool, waterfall
Beag (*beg*)	Small	Loch	Lake, fiord
Beallach (*byallach*)	Mountain pass	Machair	Fertile plain near shore
Bidean (*beejan*)	Pinnacle		
Bun	River mouth	Mam	Rounded hill
Cairn	Heap of stones used as a marker	Monadh (*monug*)	Hill, moor
		Mor	Great, extensive
Cleugh	Ravine	Ness	Headland
Cnoc (*knock*)	Hill	Rannoch	Bracken
Coille (*collu*)	Wood	Rudha (*rooa*)	Promontory
Coirre (*corru*)	Hollow in the hills	Sgur	Rocky peak
Creag	Rock	Sheugh	Ditch
Dhu	Black	Shieling	Temporary summer dwelling
Dun (*doon*)	Fort		
Eilean (*aylan*)	Island	Sloch	Pit
Garbh	Rough, rugged	Srath (*sra*)	Strath, wide valley
Gill	Ravine, watercourse	Stob	Pointed hill
Glas	Grey	Tarbert	Isthmus
Gleann (*glyown*)	Glen	Tullach	Small hill
Gorm	Blue, green	Uamh	Cave
		Uisge (*uushku*)	Water, river

APPENDIX 2

Useful Addresses

Backpackers Club
117 Swinford Road
Birmingham BH29 5SH
www.backpackersclub.co.uk

British Mountaineering Council (BMC)
177–179 Burton Road
Manchester M20 2BB
0870 010 4878
www.thebmc.co.uk

Caledonian MacBrayne Ltd
The Ferry Terminal
Gourock PA19 1QP
01475 650100
www.calmac.co.uk

Cyclists' Touring Club (CTC)
69 Meadrow
Godalming GU7 3HS
0870 873 0060
www.ctc.org.uk

Forestry Commission
231 Corstophine Road
Edinburgh EH12 7AT
0845 367 3787
www.forestry.gov.uk

Highland Hostels
1 Achluachrach
By Roybridge PH33 4AW
Fax: 01397 772411
www.highland-hostels.co.uk

Mountain Bothies Association (MBA)
PO Box 5
Giggleswick
Settle BD24 0XA
www.mountainbothies.org.uk

Mountaineering Council of Scotland (MCS)
The Old Granary
West Mill Street
Perth PH1 5QP
01738 638227
www.mountaineering-scotland.org.uk

National Trust for Scotland
28 Charlotte Square
Edinburgh EH2 4ET
0131 243 9300
www.nts.org.uk

Ordnance Survey (OS)
Romsey Road
Southampton SO16 4GW
08456 050505
www.ordnancesurvey.co.uk

Ramblers' Association Scotland
Kingfisher House
Auld Mart Business Park
Milnathort
Kinross KY13 9DA
01577 861222
www.ramblers.org.uk/scotland

RSPB (Royal Society for the Protection of Birds)
The Lodge (Head Office)
Sandy SG19 2DL
01767 68055
www.rspb.org.uk

RSPB Scotland
25 Ravelston Terrace
Edinburgh EH4 3TP
0131 311 6500

ScotWays
(Scottish Rights of Way and
Access Society)
24 Annandale Street
Edinburgh EH7 4AN
0131 558 1222
www.scotways.com

Scottish Youth Hostels Association (SYHA)
7 Glebe Crescent
Stirling FK8 2JA
0870 155 3255
www.syha.org.uk

Tourist Information Centres (TIC)
Opening times – www.visitmap.com

Craignure TIC
The Pier
Craignure
Isle of Mull PA65 6AY
01680 812377

Fort William TIC
Cameron Centre
Cameron Square
Fort William
Inverness-shire PH33 6AJ
01397 703781

Kilchoan TIC
Pier Road
Kilchoan
Acaracle
Argyll PH36 4LH
01972 510222

Oban TIC
Church Building
Argyll Square
Oban PA34 4AR
01631 563122

Strontian TIC (closed out of season)
Strontian
Acaracle
Argyll PH36 4HZ
01967 402381

Tobermory TIC (closed out of season)
Main Street
Tobermory
Isle of Mull PA75 6NU
01688 302182

Visit Scotland (Scottish Tourist Board)
PO Box 121
Livingston EH54 8AF
0845 225 5121
www.visitscotland.com

APPENDIX 3

Public Rights of Way

Great Britain has a rich heritage of footpaths dating back to prehistoric times. A network of footpaths was developed for trading purposes, especially in England and Wales, linking centres where essentials such as salt, flint and pottery were to be found. Due to the sparseness of the population in Scotland – particularly in the West Highlands – the network of paths here formed less quickly and was less developed. The original long-distance routes in Scotland were mainly military roads or drove roads. The paths frequently followed high-level routes where travelling was easier, as low-lying land was usually boggy and wooded. From the 18th century, people in England began to use footpaths for recreational purposes. The books of Jane Austin, the Brontës, Thomas Hardy and Samuel Johnson contain many references to this new activity.

Shortly after World War II the British Government wanted to clarify the case law governing the use of paths. Laws were enacted in England and Wales to rationalise the whole system. As Scotland had – and still has – its own legal system, different laws apply.

On modern Ordnance Survey (OS) 1:50,000 series maps (Landrangers) for England and Wales, rights of way are indicated by short dashed red lines for footpaths, and long dashed red lines for bridleways. The 1:25,000 series (Explorers) use short dashed green lines for right of way footpaths and long dashed green lines for bridleways. These maps carry the warning that: 'Rights of Way are not shown on maps of Scotland'.

It is often claimed that there are no rights of way in Scotland. This is not true, but rights of way are not distinguished from other paths on OS maps. On the 50,000 series tracks and paths are shown as long dashed black lines. On the 25,000 series they are shown by faint dotted black lines. In either case, these may or may not be rights of way. Current maps are of no assistance at all in giving guidance about the status of any particular track or path in Scotland.

Although the English and Welsh system of recording rights of way does not apply in Scotland, many Scottish local authority planning departments do document them. Also, the Scottish Rights of Way and Access Society keeps records of the major routes and publishes maps of some for the use of its members. Some rights of way have been signposted either by the society or by local authorities.

During the stalking season (mainly September/October, but could be at other times), signs may be displayed on some estates in Scotland advising walkers to discuss their proposed route with the estate office before proceeding. The signs imply that alternative routes may be offered to avoid shooting operations.

There is an age-old tradition in Scotland of free access to mountains and glens. (The English and Welsh have hardly enjoyed any such freedom.) This is not protected by law, but Scottish walkers and visitors to Scotland place tremendous value on the 'freedom to roam', a freedom sometimes challenged in areas where estate owners wish to 'preserve their privacy'. This state of affairs is about to change radically. In January 2003 the Scottish Parliament passed the Land Reform (Scotland) Act 2003. This received Royal Assent in March 2003 and is now in the process of implementation.

According to the Ramblers' Association Scotland website, the effect of this far-reaching legislation will be to establish a statutory right of responsible non-motorised access over most areas of land and water, including mountains, moorland, forests, farmland, coasts and river banks for passage, recreation, education and commercial activities. The access rights must be exercised in a reasonable manner and there are reciprocal obligations on land managers, both in their behaviour and in the way they manage the land. There are, of course, areas in which the new rights of way will not apply, including the curtilage of buildings and farmyards, quarries, railway property and airfields. They must draw up plans for systems of paths to give the public reasonable access. Clearly, organisations such as the Ramblers' Association Scotland and the Scottish Rights of Way and Access Society will play a great part in helping to create the new network of paths with appropriate records and maps. It has been estimated that at least £350 million will be required over the next ten years to meet the aspirations of those concerned.

So Scotland is already well on the way to having one of the best arrangements in Europe for public access to land and water for its citizens and visitors. At the time of writing it remains to be seen what will happen to the English and Welsh Countryside and Rights of Way Act 2000, with its limitations and complex and potentially bureaucratic mapping procedures.

CICERONE GUIDES TO THE BRITISH ISLES

For full information on all our British and international guides, please visit our website: **www.cicerone.co.uk**.

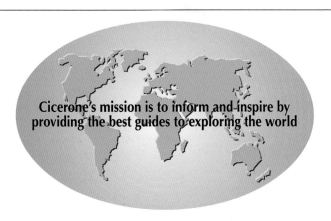

Cicerone's mission is to inform and inspire by providing the best guides to exploring the world

Since its foundation 40 years ago, Cicerone has specialised in publishing guidebooks and has built a reputation for quality and reliability. It now publishes nearly 300 guides to the major destinations for outdoor enthusiasts, including Europe, UK and the rest of the world.

Written by leading and committed specialists, Cicerone guides are recognised as the most authoritative. They are full of information, maps and illustrations so that the user can plan and complete a successful and safe trip or expedition – be it a long face climb, a walk over Lakeland fells, an alpine cycling tour, a Himalayan trek or a ramble in the countryside.

With a thorough introduction to assist planning, clear diagrams, maps and colour photographs to illustrate the terrain and route, and accurate and detailed text, Cicerone guides are designed for ease of use and access to the information.

If the facts on the ground change, or there is any aspect of a guide that you think we can improve, we are always delighted to hear from you.

Cicerone Press
2 Police Square Milnthorpe Cumbria LA7 7PY
Tel: 015395 62069 Fax: 015395 63417
info@cicerone.co.uk www.cicerone.co.uk

CICERONE